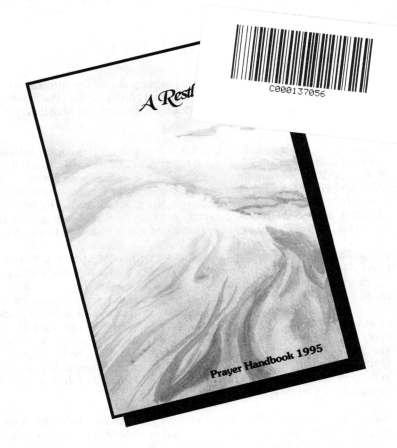

A Restl

Prayer Handbook 1995

Prayers by

**Francis Brienen &
Bernard Thorogood**

other material
selected and prepared by

Kate Compston (Editor).

C000137056

INTRODUCTION

Mission is a major theme - and Luke's gospel provides the springboard for most of the prayers - in this year's special edition of the Handbook. *A Restless Hope* celebrates the bicentenary of the London Missionary Society's formation.

We have been fortunate indeed to enlist as our writers two people intimately involved with the Council for World Mission (which is the descendant of the LMS). At the senior end, we draw on the wide experience and reflectiveness of Bernard Thorogood, now living in very active retirement in Australia. And Francis Brienen is a young woman from the Reformed Churches in the Netherlands, currently working for CWM in Britain, who is also much travelled; one of her several interests is women's development.

Bernard's prayers can be found in January, March, May, etc. - and Francis's prayers in February, April, June, and so on. My thanks to them both for providing a year of stimulating work. (I had hoped that the URC might finance occasional flights to Australia for face-to-face exchanges with Bernard, but unfortunately this application was deemed a little extravagant: however I was much helped by Bernard's prompt delivery of work at every stage.) Bernard, as editor of the 'new' history, *Gales of Change: The Story of the London Missionary Society, 1945-1977,* has willingly supplied stories of missionary endeavour from the inception of the Society to the present day - and I have been glad to include some of these accounts on the editor's (right hand) pages.

We continue to use the Four Year Lectionary to provide themes for both prayers and quotations; I have also wanted to include, as in the previous two years, ideas for small groups interested in meditation and the use of symbols in more holistic worship.

Throughout the year, prayers are asked for every CWM partner church: we also wanted to include missionary societies and churches (the latter predominantly of the Reformed tradition) with which the URC or CWM has some ongoing association. To this end, we asked both the Handbook-sponsoring churches and the twelve provinces of the URC to supply details of twinning and link arrangements with churches in other countries. I am grateful to the five provinces which responded (Yorkshire, North Western, West Midlands, Wessex and Southern): it has not been possible to make reference to every association they mentioned, nor to use more than a very few of the interesting stories supplied. But it is clear that the URC alone has links in many different parts of the world - and surely there is an opening here for the researching and collecting of anecdotes and worship material for a quite separate book ....

Another new feature this year is the collection of indexes at the back (and the 'overview' at the front). I hope these will be of considerable assistance in locating biblical passages, countries, churches, themes and so on.

All in all, I hope the prayers, stories, quotations and 'nudges towards worship' in this book will be a helpful contribution, not only to the bicentennial celebrations, but to the ongoing life of local URC and CWM partner churches - and also to those individuals and fellowships of other denominations and of far-flung parts of the world into whose hands this Handbook mysteriously falls each year ...

Once again, thanks are owing to Sara Broughton for her cover design and illustrations. I am grateful to Deborah Reynolds (Congregational Federation) who has efficiently chaired our lively Prayer Handbook Group over the year. And lastly, I want to thank all those who have offered friendship, stimulation and assistance during my three years as editor of the Handbook, and to wish to my successor, Janet Wootton, as interesting and rewarding a time as I have had.

Kate Compston.

MONTHLY THEMES

RESPONDING
1 Jan.	Christmas 2	They Found a Saviour
8 Jan.	Epiphany 1	The Cry of Warning
15 Jan.	Epiphany 2	The Fishermen's Story
22 Jan.	Epiphany 3	Mission Statement
29 Jan.	Epiphany 4	Evaluations

TRUSTING
5 Feb.	Epiphany 5	God Keeps Faith
12 Feb.	9 Easter	Parable of the Sower
19 Feb.	8 Easter	A Restless Hope
26 Feb.	7 Easter	It Is Not Easy

WITNESSING
5 Mar.	Lent 1	Temptations of Power
12 Mar.	Lent 2	A Way With Devils
19 Mar.	Lent 3	The Cost of Discipleship
26 Mar.	Lent 4	Glorious Light

SUFFERING/REJOICING
2 Apr.	Passion	A Prayer for Passiontide
9 Apr.	Palm	At the Cross of Christ
16 Apr.	Easter	The Stone Rolled Away
23 Apr.	Easter 1	The Road to Emmaus
30 Apr.	Easter 2	Peace Be With You

AFFIRMING
7 May	Easter 3	Affirming Life
14 May	Easter 4	Affirming His Friends
21 May	Easter 5	Affirming Faith
28 May	Easter 6	Affirming Presence

EMPOWERING
4 Jun.	Pentecost	The Gifts of the Spirit
11 Jun.	Trinity	Treading Down the Evils
18 Jun.	Pentecost 2	An Invitation to the Banquet
25 Jun.	Pentecost 3	God Is With Us

HEALING
2 Jul.	Pentecost 4	Healing the Lost
9 Jul.	Pentecost 5	Healing the Rejected
16 Jul.	Pentecost 6	Lover of Life
22 Jul.	Pentecost 7	Healing the Penitent
30 Jul.	Pentecost 8	Healing as Liberation

TEACHING

6 Aug.	Pentecost 9	I Will Follow You Wherever You Go
13 Aug.	Pentecost 10	Who Is My Neighbour?
20 Aug.	Pentecost 11	God of Surprises
27 Aug.	Pentecost 12	People Rise Up

CHALLENGING

3 Sep.	Pentecost 13	The Challenge of Need
10 Sep.	Pentecost 14	The Challenge of Hospitality
17 Sep.	Pentecost 15	The Challenge of Obedience
24 Sep.	Pentecost 16	The Challenge of Love

SERVING

1 Oct.	Pentecost 17	Gifts
8 Oct.	Pentecost 18	Bright and Beautiful God
15 Oct.	Pentecost 19	As Big as a Mustard Seed
22 Oct.	Pentecost Last	A Cloud of Witnesses
29 Oct.	9 Christmas	The Word Made Flesh

SAVING

5 Nov.	8 Christmas	By Christ's Salvation
12 Nov.	7 Christmas	In Christ's Constancy
19 Nov.	6 Christmas	Through Christ's Food
26 Nov.	5 Christmas	To Christ's Kingdom

IDENTIFYING

3 Dec.	Advent 1	Can't Wait!
10 Dec.	Advent 2	Messengers
17 Dec.	Advent 3	Wilderness
24 Dec.	Advent 4	Sing For Joy!
31 Dec.	Christmas 1	A Guiding Star

They Found a Saviour

How straightforward it sounds,
good, elderly people praising God for a birth.
We can do that in our churches any Sunday.
But here the insight was extraordinary,
to sense that all the ancient hopes for Israel
were coming true in this baby.

Before the press and the media and the public name,
before the Assembly has passed a resolution
or the Church Meeting has agreed,
can we recognize the Lord's presence
in his world?

God the stranger, help us to welcome you
to our land, our street, our home, our church.
God the anonymous, help us to know you
in lives that touch ours at a thousand points.
God the helpless one, may we see you
when you are cradled in a mother's arms.
God the seed, the newborn, the beginning,
help us to find our hope in you.

We thank you, pioneering God,
for the visionaries of faith
who see more clearly
and work more boldly
because they have seen you
in love, in suffering and in new life.

Pray for: **The Council for World Mission**

In 1792, William Carey issued *An Enquiry into the Obligations of Christians to use Means for the Conversion of the Heathen.*
Then he, with a small group of friends, formed the Baptist Missionary Society. In 1793, Carey sailed for India.
A letter from Carey reached Bristol in July 1794, telling of his first six weeks in Bengal. The readers were excited, they prayed and planned how they could share such a venture of faith. Dr. Ryland of Bristol, David Bogue of Gosport, James Stevens of Crown Court Church of Scotland and Mr. Hey of the Independent Church, Castle Green, Bristol, were the initial group. They were joined by John Eyre of Homerton, Matthew Wilks of Moorfields Tabernacle and John Love of the Scottish Church in Artillery Street, to plan the inaugural meetings of the London Missionary Society. The insight, enthusiasm, faith and daring of a few caught the wind of the Spirit, many gathered in support, and the LMS was launched in 1795. This cloud of witnesses encourages all our own ventures of faith today.

(Bernard Thorogood)

How many people receive sounds on their eardrums and yet hear nothing and are unable to listen? And how many people use their eyes well enough but do not really see anything?
What meditation tries to do is to free us from this paralysis of the senses, so that we can truly see and hear. Only then will the process of alienation from ourselves and others be halted ... Then our seeing will become a beholding, our hearing become a listening ...

(J. de Rooy, SJ: *Tools for Meditation*)

For a small worship group: Simeon and Anna not only saw, but 'beheld' Christ. Relax .. let one incident (personal or public) from last week surface in your mind. Ask: How was Christ present here? After five minutes of quietness, share your experiences and findings.

The Cry of Warning

How strange the figure of John appears,
the wild man from the desert,
with no appearance to commend him
and no authority of church or state to back him.
Just a cry:
  Come, repent, turn around and live.

We too know our need of forgiveness.
When we fail to meet challenges to our style of life
and bristle defensively to maintain the status quo;
when we resist debate about our position in the church,
and criticise those whose pilgrimage has joined them to a different company,

Lord, forgive us,
we are deaf so often to the cry,
Come, repent, turn around and live.

When we refuse to hear the word
because the messenger is not one of us
  with an accent we do not understand;
because the message questions what we hold sacred
or claims that faith asks for fresh sacrifices,

Lord, forgive us,
we are deaf so often to the cry,
Come, repent, turn around and live.

When the moment is critical,
a decision must be made but we fudge the issue,
the world is changing but we pretend it stays still,
a friend needs our love but we keep our door shut,

Lord, forgive us,
we are deaf so often to the cry,
Come, repent, turn around and live.

God of the prophets,
keep speaking and, by your Spirit,
help us to hear your voice.

Pray for: The Churches of Christ in Malawi (CWM)

Students from Malawi have been members at Carrs Lane URC, Birmingham, in recent years - and 'return' visits to Malawi have been undertaken by British members.

(The holy fool) is the wanderer or pilgrim who feels equally at home everywhere, yet settles down nowhere. Clothed in rags even in the winter cold ... he renounces not only material possessions but also what others regard as his sanity and mental balance. Yet thereby he becomes a channel for the higher wisdom of the Spirit.

(Bishop Kallistos Ware: *The Orthodox Way*)

... there are those who have enlarged the sphere of freedom in the face of (life's) terrible necessities. They are not simply the artists and saints and the great thinkers and doers. They are also crafts-people, trades unionists, rebellious peasants - and clowns and comedians - all of those who do not bow to what is and to those who assert what should be. Ultimately the dream that we will only approximate is this: that no one shall ever be condemned by his or her birth into a class or race or nation or gender to a life that is less than human; that everyone will choose and shape his or her existence. The good life is led by those who serve this ideal.

(Michael Harrington, *The Meaning of Life*)

Without .. openness to one another there is no genuine human relationship. Belonging together always also means being able to listen to one another.

(Gemma Corradi Fiumara: *The Other Side of Language: A Philosophy of Listening*)

The Fishermen's Story

How can an old dog learn new tricks?
As boatmen on the lake all our lives
we thought we knew it all,
and as professionals we knew when and where to fish,
but suddenly this stranger came
and led us to the catch of the year.

Surprising teacher, you point us towards
the unexpected shoal of fish,
to new hope after a night of disappointment,
and to new tasks that are full of promise.

Calling God, help us to sense your leading
so that although the church is ancient,
and the ways of discipleship have been
signposted long ago,
and although our days of service seem long
and often unproductive,
we may respond with trust to each new opportunity.
Where you see hope, may we help hope to grow.

A prayer when we are close to giving up

Unsleeping friend,
when I come to the end of my strength,
and my work has no blessing in it,
help me to remember you,
to reach for the hand of a friend
and find your love is here.

Pray for: **The China Christian Council**

What was Jesus saying when he told the fishermen to go deeper before
they let down their nets?
Perhaps that relying on shallow, surface resources will not be enough
for authentic living, and that - within a discipline of stillness and trust -
we must let down our defences and delve deep into the resources of God.
Then we might be able to chance the impossible.
Perhaps, too, he was saying that there are no quick fixes in the missionary
enterprise ... that we must enter deeply into the lives - the joys, wounds,
fears and dreams - of people, in order to be Christ to them in their situation.
A redemptive involvement with one another is a deep and self-sacrificial
involvement.
Thus his words have implications for both prayer and action. When we
'pray deep', we will be able to 'live deep'.

(Kate Compston)

In 1873, James Gilmour wrote from his solitary pioneering mission
in Mongolia:
> In the way of direct results there are absolutely none. I
> can say I have not yet seen a single Mongol anxious about his
> soul. I have seen hundreds working out their own salvation as
> they suppose - prayers, offerings, pilgrimages - but no one
> at all concerned that Christ should save him. I have got 'the
> blues' and that badly.

But he continued until 1891, when he died in service. One of his
colleagues wrote:
> I doubt if even St. Paul endured more for Christ than did
> James Gilmour. I doubt too if Christ ever received from
> human hands or human heart more loving, devoted service.

In 1900, the Boxer Rebellion caused the LMS mission in Mongolia to
be withdrawn. One of Gilmour's favourite texts was this:
> In the morning sow your seed and at evening withhold not
> your hand, for you do not know which will prosper, this
> or that, or whether both alike will be good. (Ecc. 11:6)

(Bernard Thorogood; and Lovett's *The History of the LMS*)

Mission Statement

Many organisations prepare a mission statement,
setting out the aims and principles of their work.
Luke tells us that as Jesus began his public
ministry, he took some ancient words and gave them
new life.

Fulfilling God,
when we become so used to the old words,
when the stories no longer startle us,
when the parables cease to challenge us,
and the gospel has slipped into the background of life,
may the words take flesh and blood
so that the text comes true today.

May these words take flesh:
Good news to the poor! -
poverty is not God's purpose,
destined to last forever.
May this come true today:
release for prisoners,
caught in the trap of cruel regimes
or bound by unjust laws.
May this come true today:
recovery of sight to the blind -
eyes closed by prejudice or history,
eyes shut to simple joys.
May this come true today:
the broken victims go free,
ready to start building life again.
May this come true today:
the year of the Lord's favour,
when feuds and debts are cancelled.

Fulfilling God, may we know,
in our lives and in our world,
that these words come true today.

Pray for: **The Presbyterian Church of Southern Africa (CWM)**

A Dutch doctor, Johannes Vanderkemp, was the first missionary appointed by the LMS to serve in South Africa. He quickly discovered that the colonists there were oppressing the tribes, driving them off their land and reducing them to slavery. As he attempted to teach the Kaffirs and Hottentots, so the colonists persecuted him. From Vanderkemp's journal, 1801:

> June 30th: The colonists complained that government protected the Hottentots and Kaffirs and encouraged them to rob and murder the colonists; that they were instructed by us in reading, writing and religion, and thereby put upon an equal footing with the Christians; especially that they were admitted in the church of Graaff Reinet ...

(Bernard Thorogood: and Lovett's *The History of the LMS*)

In the city, God through Christ reveals himself as love through the body of Christ, to liberate, heal and renew. The homeless, disadvantaged and the hungry are his concern and therefore our concern. Thus where we are whole, we are called to bring wholeness. This is not only spiritual, but physical as well ... We will not become credible until we feed the hungry, offer accommodation and launch an assault against oppression.

(Peter Jackson, Presbyterian Church of Southern Africa; *NewShare.*)

Memory has great staying power. A father passed on to his son this story fifty years after its occurrence ... During his training for the ministry he noticed missionaries meeting with no nationals apparently being present. He asked a friend: 'Why are they meeting without us?' The reply: 'They are deciding our destiny for us.' The son now tells the story to those who have ears to hear. Isn't the proper role of the Church in Christ's mission rather to *share* in the destiny of others?
Mission is not simply doing good for others; it is helping them to discover in Christ what they can do themselves.

(*Mission: Commitment to God's Hopeful Vision*, Presbyterian Church of the U.S.A.)

Evaluations

While pollsters mark us down on clipboard sheets
and TV ratings detail what we view,
here stands this searching one who meets
our eyes and tests to see if we are true.
Is this the champion, winner in the race
of market forces? Who has made the grade?
You turn us upside down. In you we face
the judgement on all earthly forms of trade.

Judge eternal,
you know how we have come to accept
the standards of our culture and our day,
how we have been shaped by
the popular notion of success,
so that we fail to see as you see.
We pray for insight
to see significance in the ordinary,
        greatness in self-giving,
        splendour in faithfulness,
        glory in tenderness.

As we remember that poor widow in the temple
we pray that we may learn
from the generosity of the poor,
from their patience in bearing pain
and their dignity in sorrow.
Teach us, as you know our hearts,
to depend on you when the world is shaking
and our little security is swept away
so that we may be kept by faith, in faith,
available for you, among your people.

Pray for: **The Union of Welsh Independents (CWM)**

Costly giving was the experience of pioneer missionaries in Madagascar:
In a Welsh seminary at Neuaddlwyd, two young men heard a call to service and responded. They were David Jones and Thomas Bevan. With their families they sailed in 1818 and stayed at Mauritius until they could reach Tamatave on the east coast of Madagascar. The Jones family arrived there on 20 November, and the Bevans on 6 January 1819. Instead of a happy reunion, Mrs. Jones and her child had died of fever and David was seriously ill. The three Bevans quickly fell victim and died. So of the party of six only one was left, 'and he at death's door'.

That might have been the end of the enterprise, but it was just the beginning. David Jones recovered and in 1820 reached Antananarivo, where he was received by ruling chief Radama 1, and was invited to remain. A new group of workers was sent from England. David Griffiths and John Jeffreys were ministers, Thomas Brooks a carpenter, John Canham a currier and shoemaker, George Chick a blacksmith, and Thomas Rowlands a weaver.

(Bernard Thorogood, based on Lovett's *History of the LMS*)

The proportion of our wealth that we give is the critical issue - not the raw amount. The poor widow gave her capital rather than a self-righteous tithe. Jesus is striking out against the rich. He also affirms the Jubilee attitude of the poor widow. This is upside-down Jubilee when the poor give with greater sincerity than the rich ... We obviously cannot conclude that the Christian's economic practice is a peripheral fringe of the gospel ... Conversion which does not involve economic change is not authentic conversion.

(Donald B. Kraybill: *The Upside-Down Kingdom*)

We know that God's arithmetic is somewhat odd.
When you subtract by giving away, you get more.
When you seek to hoard, somehow you lose out.

(Bishop Desmond Tutu, South Africa)

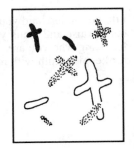

Jeremiah 13:1-11
1 Corinthians 2:1-5
Luke 5:33-39

God Keeps Faith

I do not understand you, God,
where people are stubborn
and turn away from you t
o worship other gods,
you speak through your prophets
the warning words of love.

I do not understand you,
God, where people want rules
and clear directions
to follow where you go,
you talk of wine and garments
and the joyful feast of faith.

I do not understand you, God,
where people impress with eloquence
and superior wisdom,
you send a trembling apostle
without big words
to preach your way of truth.

Holy God,
you pass my understanding.
When I pursue false truths
you do not let me go.
When I want laws to live by,
you dance into my heart.
When I want human wisdom,
you speak your words of power.

I do not understand you, God,
but I praise and thank you
for being who you are,
for keeping faith with me.

Pray for: **The Waldensian Church in Italy**

The Waldensian Church is the oldest Protestant church in Europe, going back to the 12th century. The followers of Peter Waldo of Lyon lived a life of poverty, insisting on the right of both men and women to preach the gospel and bring the Scriptures to the people. They were soon excommunicated by the Church of Rome, but the movement spread widely throughout Europe. Then they were cruelly persecuted: numbers shrank and the Church survived only in the Cottian Alps, Turin. Not until the 19th century were they granted civil rights; this enabled them to evangelize and grow once again.

The URC-Waldensian Fellowship was formed in 1981, after 50 people from the North Western Province visited Torre Pellice. Seven more groups have since visited different regions, and parties of Italians have made return visits to England. Ministerial exchanges have also taken place.

(Ruth Cowhig, Sale; North Western Province, URC)

Philosophy lives in words, but truth wells up into our lives in ways that exceed formulation. There is in the living act of perception always something which glimmers and twinkles and will not be caught, and for which reflection comes too late.

(William James: *The Varieties of Religious Experience*)

Mystery - a consequence of living.
The inescapable dynamic force
At our centres.

(Peter Brock, Australia; in *Your Will be Done*, CCA)

... he does not wish that men should love him more than anything Because he died; he only wishes they would hear him sing.

(Stevie Smith: 'The Airy Christ', *Selected Poems.*)

12 February

Proverbs   3:1-8
1 Corinthians   4:8-16
Luke   8:4-15

Parable of the Sower

Let us pray for peace in the world,
the time of God's shalom:

> In the times until then we pray
> dear God,
> that some glimpses will remain
> of the great story of your life.
> We pray that the weeds will not overgrow
> your great message of love.
> Let there be places of memory and of hope.

And forgive us -
when we boast in your name,
when we show off with your word,
when we distort your image.
If the church has to be
ploughed under in the great field,
let it be so.
But bless with the seed that you are sowing
> the world that is longing,
> the world that is crying out
and carry your people safely
> through the winds of history
> until your kingdom come.

Christ the Sower,
patient and loving,
magnificent and awesome,
so near and yet so hidden,
we pray to you:
have mercy!

Based on a prayer by W Barnard (1967)

Pray for: **The Latin American Council of Churches**

To garden with others is an expression of solidarity; that is what being 'campaneras' is all about. Gardening is visioning, dreaming, and futuring ... But I cannot bring about the new earth by myself, because a new earth demands that we look at the universe in which we are immersed, we must look for the new we are called to bring forth. We must see what is old and decadent and death-giving ... The garden I inherited from my mother has become for me the whole of creation. We all need to join together to live as 'campaneras' and tend the global garden ... We must .. make real connections between the gardens of El Salvador, Central America and the whole world. I am one with my nation just as the plants and flowers are one with the soil. But the soil of El Salvador has been plundered, and there is almost nothing for us to inherit.

(Maria Benavides, El Salvador: *My Mother's Garden is a New Creation.*)

Because of our faith in Christ and in humankind, we must apply our efforts to the construction of a more just and humane world. And I want to declare emphatically: such a world is possible. To create this new society, we must present outstretched, friendly hands, without hatred, without rancour - even as we show great determination, never wavering in the defence of truth and justice. Because we know that seeds are not sown with clenched fists. To sow we must open our hands.

(Adolfo Perez Esquivel, receiving the Nobel Peace Prize.)

For a worship group: Ecology has been called the study of the 'all-togetherness of everything'. Focussing on a tree (real or pictured), think about how different forms of life relate to, and depend on, its presence. What hinders and encourages its growth? Why are trees called the 'lungs of the planet'? What implications are there for the way we relate to trees and other life forms? Perhaps create a Tree of Life collage - or write a prayer that celebrates the 'all-togetherness' of God's world.

A Restless Hope

Do not give us rest, Lord,
while people are hungry
and we are rich.
As long as justice is a dream
press us on
and do not give us rest.

Do not give us peace, Lord,
while people live in fear
and we are safe.
As long as hatred stifles love
stir us up
and do not give us peace.

Do not give us comfort, Lord,
while people are desperate
and we are well.
As long as lives are lived in pain
disturb us
and do not give us comfort.

But give us hope to share, O Christ,
hope that disturbs and stirs and shakes,
the hope of Job,
the hope of the lame,
a hope of new life
beyond the pain.
Until all find comfort
and peace
and rest,
Christ, give us hope to share.

Pray for: **The United Congregational Church of Southern Africa (CWM)**

There is no way at the moment, given the impersonal character of most of the liturgies of established and mainstream churches, that the stories of the victims of abuse, of homelessness, of racist discrimination, are heard into speech, even though they may be given a nod in the prayers of intercession. The binding functions of true ecclesia are characterized by verbs of connection - by hearing, listening, responding, communing, reaching out and touching, by the mutuality of committing, cherishing, remembering and healing.

(Mary Grey: *The Wisdom of Fools?*)

Power 'at the top' and power 'on the ground'

'When elephants fight, the grass suffers.' (Old African saying)
It is important for us to understand that when we raise the question of peace, we do not only speak about the arms race at the top, but we also look at the grass, which suffers when elephants fight. I am one who belongs to the grassroots. That is why I can speak about the *whole* human race. And what is the elephant fight all about? What role do we play in relation to the grass which suffers? Where is our personal involvement in the real struggle for peace?
We need desperately a circle of friends at all levels, from the grass to the stem of the grass, up to the elephants, in order to develop a global understanding of the problems and not be narrow in our approach.
I see my role at this moment in the history of my country, Zimbabwe, as that of making myself available at the lowest level of my community. I have to help people, especially women, to articulate their situation and ask the right questions of ourselves, so that we can search for relevant answers to our problems. My heart is heavy. I am involved in the struggle for life in rural poor Africa. The elephants destroy this life which I am struggling for. Therefore I need you, sisters, to stand beside me in this struggle.

(Sithembiso Nyoni, Zimbabwe)

It Is Not Easy

It is not easy, God, to keep believing
that you are always with us.
In our times, multiply our trust.

It is not easy, God, to keep believing
that people can change.
In our times, multiply our love.

It is not easy, God, to keep believing
that the world is in your hand.
In our times, multiply our faith.

It is not easy, God, to keep believing
that injustice is not merely a fact of life.
In our times, multiply our anger.

It is not easy, God, to keep believing
that your kingdom will come.
In our times, multiply our hope.

Jesus who fed the multitudes
with five loaves and two fish,
**multiply our faith, hope and love,
and may your presence
be felt among us.**

Pray for: **CEVAA (Communauté Évangelique d'Action Apostolique)**

There's a piece of bread travelling through the world that no one has yet succeeded in finishing, and the more you eat the more it accumulates: we are the crumbs of Bethsaida, we, the five cold yellow loaves harvested from the apostles' haver-sacks. When you are asked for something you think you're unable to give, remember us, the pieces of bread left over in the twelve baskets.

(Luigi Santucci: *Wrestling with Christ*)

When many persons have access to participation in the structures of decision-making, there is often an explosion of energy ... The charismatic authority of Jesus that enabled him to preach, heal and work among the people was not something he kept to himself. Thus, for instance, in the story of the 5000, we hear that he involved the disciples and the people in the feeding ... Charisma becomes a gift of empowerment for others rather than one for domination and manipulating others.

(Letty M. Russell in *Feminist Theology: A Reader*)

You placed me in the world to be its salt.
I was afraid of committing myself,
Afraid of being stained by the world.
I did not want to hear what 'they' might say.
And my salt dissolved as if in water.
      You placed me in the world to be its light.
      I was afraid of the shadows,
      Afraid of the poverty.
      I did not want to know other people.
      And my light slowly faded away.
You placed me in the world to live in community.
Thus you taught me to love,
To share in life,
To struggle for bread and for justice,
Your truth incarnate in my life.
So be it, Jesus.

(Peggy M. de Cuehlo, Uruguay)

Temptations of Power

We all know something of power,
if only the power of words,
the power of knowledge,
the power of love.

You, Lord Jesus, knew great power,
to heal, to transform,
to proclaim the reign of God.
So you met great temptations.
The wrong way, glittering and possible, was open;
you could rule if you chose,
in majesty and wonder,
more victorious than Alexander,
more imperial than Caesar.
  But you said No,
   simply, decisively, for ever, for us.

We pray for the Church, tempted like its Head.
When the Church seeks political power,
  Jesus, stay with us.
When the Church longs to become wealthy,
  Jesus, speak to us.
When the Church strives to impress with splendour,
  Jesus, give us simplicity.
When the Church wanders from the way of sacrifice,
  Jesus, hold us.
When the Church listens to the call for cheap grace,
  Jesus, keep us always in your way.

Holy Spirit of God, enable us to respond to temptation
with the strength of your word within us,
so that we may hold firm to our calling
and take your better way in faithfulness.

Pray for: **The Christian Conference of Asia**

In his play 'The Gold Crowned Jesus,' Korean author and poet Kim Chi Ha depicts Christ as a statue which is adorned with a golden crown by those who venerate materialism and are absorbed with their own power and position. It takes a poor leper to understand the agony of the imprisoned Christ. He is moved by compassionate desire to set Christ free:

Leper: What can be done to free you,
Jesus, make you live again so that
you can come to us?

Jesus: My power alone is not enough.
People like you must help to
liberate me. Those who seek only
the comforts, wealth, honour, and
power of this world, who wish entry to the kingdom of heaven
for themselves only and ignore the poor and less fortunate,
cannot give me life again. Neither can those who have never
suffered loneliness, who remain silent while injustice is done and
so acquiesce to it, who are without courage. It is the same with
those without courage who are unwilling to resist such evildoers
as dictators and other tyrants who inflict great suffering on the
weak and poor. Prayer alone is not enough; it is necessary also to
act. Only those, though very poor and suffering like yourself,
who are generous in spirit and seek to help the poor and
wretched can give me life again. You have helped give me life
again. You removed the gold crown from my head and so freed
my lips to speak. People like you will be my liberators.

(Kim Chi Ha: *The Gold Crowned Jesus*)

Neither let us be slandered from our duty by false accusations against us,
nor frightened from it by menaces of destruction. Let us have faith that
right makes might and, in that faith and to that end, let us dare to do our
duty as we understand it.

(Source untraced)

A Way With Devils

*We do not talk readily of devils, as people
did in Jesus' day, but we too know that our
human personality can be swamped, taken over,
as though possessed.*

Good Spirit of God
whatever possessed me,
when I blurted out that angry word,
when I slapped my noisy child
when I chased that erotic dream
when I resigned out of sudden frustration
when I thought of suicide
what possessed me?

Good Spirit of God
whatever possessed us,
when the crowd shouted 'Barabbas!',
when nationalism became a fever,
when racism gripped our hearts
and justice fled.
What possessed us?

Healing Spirit of God
we pray for all who are in the grip of evil,
who in despair see no light at all,
who in addiction find no release,
who in bitterness know no mercy,
who in fear cannot love.
Heal, inspire, release, renew,
Spirit of the living God.

Pray for: **The Pacific Conference of Churches**

In my last letter to you, dated September 5, 1827, I was under the disagreeable necessity of informing you of a division that had taken place occasioned by the madness of two men, Teao and Hue, who pretended they had visions from heaven and that they were raised up to introduce their former customs into the worship of God.

(David Darling, missionary in Tahiti, 1828)

This cult, known as Mamaia, combined ecstatic behaviour with pre-Christian customs and spread during the 1830s. It died out in 1841.

I can tell you in this idle solitude there are a thousand battles with Satan. It is much easier to fight against the incarnate devil, that is, against men, than against spiritual wickedness in the heavenly places. Often I fall and am lifted again by God's right hand.

(Martin Luther's letters from the Wartburg, 1521)

(The prayer of thanksgiving) is one of the ways we can escape the clutch of the past ... Thanksgiving detaches me from the past and anchors me in the present. It is not only an expression of gratitude, it is an affirmation of faith. Even the evils of the past, the fear, the guilt, the humiliation, the rejection experienced long ago but still alive in memory, can be matter for thanksgiving for those who believe that God is at work, healing the hurt, bringing good out of evil, liberating the good imprisoned by fear or chained to buried memories.

(Christopher Bryant: *The River Within*)

We can now recognise that the fate of the soul is the fate of the social order; that if the spirit within us withers, so too will all the world we build about us.

(Theodore Roszak: *Where the Wasteland Ends*)

The Cost of Discipleship

*Within most of us there is an inward
conversation as we begin to follow the way
of Jesus.*

Jesus, we would follow you.
You fulfil all the promises,
you lead in humility,
you do not run from danger.

> But do you know the cost?
> The broken bread is not a delicacy,
> it is rough pilgrim food.
> The cross is not a trinket
> but pain, disgrace and loss.
> We will meet beside the tomb.

Yes, you are the one who knows life and death,
you understand loneliness and sorrow;
you face them to open the way
to new birth and true peace.
We would follow you.

> Come, then, but do not carry
> too much baggage from your past
> or fixed notions about your future.
> Come in freedom and faith.

It's not easy, Jesus. We are slow learners.
Have mercy, pioneer of the way.
Have mercy, friend of the oppressed.
Have mercy, bearer of the cross.

Pray for: **The Kiribati Protestant Church (CWM)**

A Polynesian missionary pays the price, 1842:
Next they attacked the two teachers. Lasalo, however, did not die straight away. He had been struck but was not yet dead. He ran towards the chief who called out, 'Come, come quickly.' He prostrated himself before the chief, saying, 'O Matuka, have you no sympathy for us?' And the chief replied, 'I have some feeling for you.' The chief stood up and moved aside and another man stepped forward to kill Lasalo, but he ran into the sea and they shoved him under the water. Still he survived. Again he was pushed under but even then he would not die. He was left to float in the sea until he was washed ashore on an islet. He climbed the rocky shore, and when the people realised that he was not dead, they paddled over in a canoe. He had just finished praying when they reached him and they seized him and flung him from the rocks. So he died.

(Eds. R.G. and M. Crocombe: *The Works of Ta'unga*)

Alfred Sadd was a young missionary in Kiribati (the Gilbert Islands) when the Japanese attacked in 1942. He refused to leave with other expatriots, was caught and taken to Tarawa, where, with a group of others, he was shot on 15 October. Their memorial says:

    Standing unarmed to their posts,
    they matched brutality with gallantry
    and met death with fortitude.

(Bernard Thorogood)

How much the rice must suffer
under the pestle;
But, after the pounding,
it comes out
white like cotton.

The same thing often happens
to people in this world:
Misfortune's workshop
turns them
to polished jade.

(Ho Chi Minh, Vietnam)

26 March

Exodus   34:29-35
2 Corinthians   3:4-18
Luke   9:28-36

Glorious Light

*On a mountainside Jesus was clothed in light,
revealed as the Christ, fulfiller of God's purpose.*

Jesus with Moses -
all that was holy and loving in the law,
all that pointed to a just society,
all that showed the character of God
was there in Jesus.
      May your light shine on our traditions.

Jesus with Elijah -
all that the prophets proclaimed,
all that was passionate for truth,
all that declared the greatness of God
was there in Jesus.
      May your light shine on our faith.

We too need glimpses of glory,
when we doubt the calling of Christ,
when work is both demanding and dull
and no healing seems to happen.
      Come as light and vision
      come as glory and joy
      come as confidence and hope
      and show us Christ.

A Prayer for Mothering Sunday

Motherhood was never easy,
not for Mary, not for us.
There's longing in it, waiting, pain,
hard work and tight budgets.
But you, creating God, come that way,
lighting with glory the bond of trust
and humble devotion.
Speak to us, God, through our mothers
that we may know your steadfast love.

Pray for: **The Presbyterian Church of India (CWM)**

Churches in the North Western Province have links with various churches in India. Pray for deepening friendships.

... the spiritual is not the extraordinary but the ordinary understood at depth.

(Elizabeth Brimelow: *In and Out the Silence*)

Our mundane experiences contain all the stuff of holiness and human growth in grace. Our world is rife with messages and signatures of the Spirit ... We fail so often to recognize the light that shines through the tiny chinks and the dusty panes of our daily lives. We are too busy to name the event that is blessed in its ordinariness, holy in its uniqueness, and grace-filled in its underlying challenge.

(Joan Puls: *Every Bush is Burning*)

Everyday we cross the same street or the same garden, every afternoon our eyes meet the same red wall, built with bricks and urban time. Suddenly, in a day like all others, the street leads to another world, the garden has just been planted, the tired wall is covered with signs. We had never seen them, and now we are surprised .. we are spellbound, suspended in the middle of the immobile afternoon.

(Octavio Paz: *O Arco e a Lira*)

... all things were new and all the creation gave another smell unto me than before, beyond what words can utter ...

(George Fox: *Journal*)

The power of the miracle is the power of imagination.

(Feuerbach)

A Prayer for Passiontide

Compassionate God,
we pray for those who have no land,
who work the fields of others,
who pick the fruit
but do not know its taste.

We pray for those who have no home,
who are displaced, uprooted,
their homes destroyed
by landlords and warlords.

We pray for those who have lost their children,
for whom there is no future,
their sons taken to war,
their daughters sold into slavery.

> **May their dreams be not broken,**
> **May their spirits be not crushed,**
> **May their lives be not forgotten.**

Instead, break our dreams of 'more', O God,
and crush our spirit of greed,
we for whom enough is never enough,
who do not understand the tears of the poor,
whose way of life perpetuates the grip of suffering.

Christ, who went before us,
help us to remember in your passion
all those who suffer.
Help us to remember in your passion
the promise of justice,
the promise of peace,
the promise of new life.
You who in your life on earth
cried out to God, pray for us now.

Pray for: **The United Church in Jamaica and the Cayman Islands (CWM)**

The parables had a sizzling sting for the religious heavy-weights ... You are like the tenants of a vineyard who refused to give one of the owner's servants some of the wine from his own vineyard. You killed other servants he sent and finally you had the daring audacity to kill his only son. Suddenly the tables are turned. The owner will give that vineyard to others. This upside-down theme of reversal permeates other parables. The unexpected happens. The religious leaders forfeit their kingdom card. Sinners have a seat at the party.

(Donald B. Kraybill: *The Upside-Down Kingdom*)

About an hour's drive from Kingston, the Hillside Farmers' Association (a partner organization of Christian Aid) tries to help former sugar cane workers make the tough transition from paid employees to self-employed farmers. But Jamaica's foreign debt means that inputs like fertiliser, seeds and technology, are increasingly expensive. For example, in 1989, Christian Aid approved a grant for a tractor. Immediately afterwards, the Jamaican currency was devalued. The price of the tractor in Jamaican dollars increased by almost a third! Because of the foreign debt, a lot more time, energy and money were required to get the tractor. Talk of debt forgiveness within the IMF is gaining wider credence. But some take exception to the way in which the word 'forgiveness' frames the problem. 'We are not asking for forgiveness,' said Peta-Anne Baker of the Association of Development Agencies in Kingston, 'because we did not commit a sin and the banks are not God.'

(Christian Aid: *Highlight on Jamaica*, 1990)

... one has to take sides, to cast one's lot with the poor and oppressed ... to be a Christian one must be prepared to be misunderstood, to be maligned and to be branded a 'subversive' ... it is only when we start to feel and identify ourselves with others that we become alive.

(Fr. Manny Lahoz, Philippines: a letter from prison.)

At the Cross of Christ

To your cross we bring our grief
for the hurt that has deformed us,
the wounds that have not healed.

> To your cross we bring our guilt
> for the pain that we have caused others,
> the injuries we have inflicted.

To your cross we bring our anger
for the violence caused by others,
the evil deeds they do not repent.

> To your cross we bring our fear
> of the hatred we have stored up inside,
> the violence too frightening to acknowledge

**Brother Christ,
who suffers with us
in you are known
all grief and guilt, all anger and fear.
From your cross restore and renew us
and help us to live
as forgiven and forgiving people.**

Pray for: **The United Church of Canada**

In 1983, the Royal Academy in London exhibited the Cimabue crucifix, a vast wooden structure, painted in the thirteenth century and severely damaged in the Florence flood of 1966 ... Before it was damaged, the watcher's gaze was drawn upwards by the curve of Christ's body to his eyes, and from there to the figure of God watching over him. The flood damaged that natural upward movement, broke it and obscured it - now our gaze remains fixed on the half obliterated face of the suffering man, his eyes closed in secret and terrible pain. God is no longer part of the picture ... If God is there now, he is in the broken man, not hovering overhead uninvolved.

(Richard MacKenna: *God For Nothing*)

There will be detectable cruciformity in the missionary's life. One would expect brokenness for none of us is whole and perfect. All brokenness, however, is not cruciform ... Cruciform brokenness is that which we offer to Christ on behalf of others, and becomes by God's grace a sign of the Kingdom. The marks of sacrifice do not come by human achievement, but through Christ's receiving of an offered life.

Are we as a Church ready to undergo the radical conversion to Christ's mission in our day? Any reading of the Gospels, any contemplation of the hopeful vision from the shards of brokenness amidst which we sit, any pondering of the Church, leads to the certain conclusion that we are being asked to enter more deeply into the cross in order to participate in God's mission to free all creation to fullness of life and joy.

(From *Mission: Commitment to God's Hopeful Vision*,
Presbyterian Church of the USA)

A man took a broken plate to the restorers.
'Do you want it mended the English way or the Chinese way?' he was asked. 'The English way is to make an invisible mend. The Chinese way is to mark the breaks with gold - for brokenness is part of the history of the plate.'

16 April

Exodus	14:15-22
Romans	6:3-11
Luke	24:1-11

The Stone Rolled Away

When the broken come to wholeness,
when the wounded come to healing,
when the frightened come to trusting,

the stone has been rolled away.

When the lonely find friendship,
when the hurt find new loving,
when the worried find peace,

the stone has been rolled away.

When we share instead of taking,
when we stroke instead of striking,
when we join around the table,

the stone has been rolled away.

The stone has been rolled away!
In you, Christ Jesus,
love breaks through hatred,
hope breaks through despair,
life breaks through death.
Hallelujah, Christ is risen!

Pray for: **The Nauru Congregational Church (CWM)**

Hope is the prospect of the radically new. It is the breaking in of what we had never even dreamed of, a fulfilment utterly beyond our power to conceive.

(H.A. Williams: *True Resurrection*)

> Woman, in a dark and quiet
> corner of the home, patient,
> resigned, waiting for this
> sublime hour in which a just
> revolution would break her yoke
> and untie her wings.

(Ana Betancourt, Cuba)

We praise the God whose image is our own,
the mystery within our flesh and bone,
the womanspirit moving through all time
in prophecy, Magnificat and dream.
Forgiving what is past, we seek the new:
a finer justice, and a peace more true,
the promise of empowering for our day
when men and women roll the stone away.

(Shirley Erena Murray, New Zealand; stanzas 2 and 4 of 'Of women, and of women's hopes we sing' from *In Every Corner Sing*, Hope Publishing Company, Carol Stream, IL 60188)

Response after each couplet: **We shall sing Magnificat and know the truth of Easter.**

When our sisters discover their value
despite their humiliations: **We shall sing ...**
When our sisters grow tall and walk together,
unnerving the powerful with their dignity: **We shall sing ...**
When our sisters tell their 'idle tale'
and are believed and honoured: **We shall sing ...**
When our sisters know God within them
and see their natures affirmed in Hers: **We shall sing ...**

(Kate Compston)

23 April

2 Kings   7:1-16
Revelations   19:6-9
Luke   24:13-35

The Road to Emmaus

Friend who walks our way,
    before the day is over
    change the focus of our seeing
    and help us to be aware of your presence.

Friend who walks our way,
    before the day is over
    capture our hearts and minds
    and help us to hear you in the voices of unexpected people.

Friend who walks our way,
    before the day is over
    show us the path to follow
    and help us to support those who have lost their way.

Friend who walks our way,
    before the day is over,
    fill us with your love
    and may your reflection be seen in us
    as we break bread together.

Friend who walks our way,
    before the day is over,
    make yourself known to us
    and we will sing your praise
    and shout with many voices:
    Hallelujah, our God reigns.

Pray for: **The Evangelical Presbyterian Church in Portugal**

The West Midlands Province (URC) is seeking to establish a link with the Evangelical Presbyterian Church in Portugal.

The passage describing the journey of two disciples to Emmaus has become a key passage for missiological reflection ... Jesus as the companion was recognized in brokenness. One can retrace Jesus' story to discover that this is part and parcel of his life and mission from the beginning. He is broken on the cross, in the midst of fractured lives; he summed up his life's meaning in sacramental elements of broken bread and poured out wine; he broke the bread available in the wilderness to feed the hungry crowd; he refused to turn stones into bread but rather became bread available for consuming by empty lives; he began life in a family away from home and experienced the life of a refugee in a broken community. 'He learned obedience through what he suffered' (Heb. 5:8), therefore he became the eternal model of the companion in brokenness.

(The Manner of Persons in Mission: *Mission: Commitment to God's Hopeful Vision,* Presbyterian Church of the USA)

Food is heaven.
As you cannot go to heaven alone,
Food is to be shared. Food is heaven.
When food passes your throat
You accept heaven in your body. Food is heaven.
Ah! Food is something that must be shared.

(Kim Chi Ha, Korea: *Declaration of Conscience*)

The Latin languages preserve an intuition which seems to be absent from English. Their words for 'knowledge' and 'taste' come from the same root. 'Sapere', in Latin, means both to 'know' and to 'have flavour'. In my language (Portuguese), 'saber' - to know, and 'sabor' - taste. Eating and knowing have the same origin. To know something is to feel its taste
...

(Rubem A. Alves: *The Poet, The Warrior, The Prophet*)

Peace Be With You

Christ, who stood among the disciples,
showing them your hands and feet
to take away their doubts,
we welcome you.

Christ, who met with the disciples,
eating in their presence
to make them see,
we welcome you.

Christ, who spoke to the disciples,
opening their minds
to reveal God's promise,
we welcome you.

You,
who stand among us,
meet with us,
speak to us,
have mercy on us.

If we are ruled by doubt, **have mercy on us.**
If we live in fear, as if you are still dead, **have mercy on us.**
If we fail to be your hands and feet, **have mercy on us.**
If we read scripture, but do not grasp the gospel, **have mercy on us.**
If we do not forgive as we are forgiven, **have mercy on us.**

(Silence)

We receive the gift of grace, from him who promised grace.
We receive the gift of peace, from him who promised peace.
We receive the gift of life, from him who died
and lives again.
Thanks be to God.

Pray for: **The Reformed Churches in the Netherlands (CWM)**

I wondered what hope there is for Penrhys ('built' - says John Morgan - 'without heart or purpose.') Today John answered the question: 'If there is any hope, there it is,' as he pointed at the children and young people who had just performed a play in the worship. After the service had ended, some remained seated in the chapel. Michael, 12 years old and part of the musical choir, came back in and started singing all by himself. He sang beautifully, with no shame at all. We sat and listened. It was a special moment. When he had finished, John turned to me with tears in his eyes and said, 'He can't read, you know!'

(Francis Brienen, Netherlands, now in Britain: *YouthShare*)

Like an archaeologist seeking traces of his own past, Adrian Cojocarita has been digging the black soil of the village where he was born, rooting out fragments of his old home in the hope he can make use of them to start his family's life afresh. Fragments are all he can find. His family and all his neighbours in Ghermanesti, near Bucharest, Romania, were ordered to dismantle their own homes eight years ago as part of a campaign of forced removals by the communist regime. With his wife and son, Mr. Cojocarita is using weekends off to build a new house alongside the grave of the old one. The walls are made from cement blocks, with the excavated bricks plugging the gaps.

(Julian Borger: *The Guardian*, 2 March 1994)

I invite you to believe me when I say future.
If you don't believe in my eyes
believe in the anguish of a shout
believe in the earth .. the rain .. the sap ..
There are twenty thousand new seeds
in the valley overnight ....
Our shackles are already broken
there's patience and more where that came from ...
I invite you to believe me when I say future.

(Silvio Rodriguez, Cuba)

7 May

Exodus   16:4-15
1 Corinthians   8:1-13
John   6:35-40

Affirming Life

So much belittles human lives,
making them seem cheap and sordid.
Hourly, the world over, children die
through neglect, poverty, disease
and they are so readily forgotten.

> **Bread of life, challenge us
> to share bread with the hungry.**

Hourly, the world over, people are oppressed
by economic forces until despair takes over
and life no longer seems worth living.

> **Bread of life, challenge us to find space
> for each one to know life in its fulness.**

But hour by hour there are those who find
a new job, a friendship,
a kindness which brings relief,
a bright hope like rain in the desert.
Then life becomes again a precious gift.

> **Bread of life, challenge us always
> to welcome others to your feast.**

And hour by hour the Spirit comes with power
to gather the family of Christ,
to bring faith to birth,
and so to bind together
our days and nights
with the very life of God.

> **Bread of life, we praise you
> for sustaining all living things,
> for giving meaning to each one
> and light for each day.
> We praise you for the life you give,
> not counted in hours
> but in depth of love and height of joy.**

Pray for: **The Presbyterian Church of the USA;**
The Disciples of Christ, USA;
The United Church of Christ, USA,
and the Reformed Church in America.

Churches in the Southern and Yorkshire Provinces (URC) have link or twinning arrangements with churches in the USA.

(When we pray the Lord's Prayer) are we asking, with Luke, for the reassurance of 'daily bread' - strength to keep going in a world which we expect to continue much as it is now? Or are we, with Matthew, pressing urgently to be given today 'the bread of tomorrow' - the Messianic feast for the poor that is a sign of a totally different world order?
On the whole, we have chosen the first approach ... we pray for spiritual stamina day by day ... we celebrate a spiritual kingdom of power and glory that somehow authorizes and blesses the systems we presently live under. Many Christians in the poorest parts of our world pray quite differently. They pray for real food, but they are also hungry for justice; they long for freedom from the intolerable burdens the international debt places on them, and look to that biblical time of jubilee when debts are remitted and justice prevails. They look, on this earth, for (God's) kingdom and power ...

(Janet Morley: *Bread of Tomorrow*, SPCK/Christian Aid)

Let's Celebrate, Inc., a coalition of thirty-three religious communities organized to fight hunger and homelessness in Jersey City .. coordinates an emergency food network consisting of nineteen food pantries and four soup kitchens. The Square Meal (a soup kitchen in Jersey City's Central Square) serves thousands of meals a year. Steve, a thirty year old homeless man, eats regularly at the Square Meal. He says, 'Most of the time, people who are homeless don't have anywhere to eat. If they (Let's Celebrate, Inc.) didn't do this, we would starve, eat out of a grabage can, or steal.' Aaki Mohamed is grateful for the food, but he points out another benefit of participating in a sit-down meal once a day. Mohamed says, 'Breaking bread together makes us feel stronger.'

(*Profile in Mission:* Reformed Church in America)

Affirming His Friends

When we hear of the first disciples
we recognise a very average group,
so slow to grasp what you were saying,
so willing to run away from danger
yet so quick to claim privilege in the Kingdom.
A pretty average lot.
Like us.

> **But you chose them, pioneer of the way,**
> **and you called them friends.**

We often doubt our own discipleship,
unsure whether we have done God's will,
growing deaf to the challenge of the gospel,
irritated by our companions on the way
and sceptical about the reign of God.

> **But you choose us, pilgrim Lord,**
> **and you call us friends.**

May we live as your friends,
seeking to know what is in your mind,
staying with you in all weathers,
unafraid to ask the awkward questions,
knowing that laughter and tears
are all part of this friendship.
Keep calling us, today and everyday,
to live in that love
which is the sign of your presence
and the healing power for all humanity.

> **The strength is not in our response**
> **but in your choosing,**
> **not in our obedience,**
> **but in your gift of acceptance,**
> **king of the cross.**

Pray for: **The United Church of Papua New Guinea and the Solomon Islands (CWM)**

James Chalmers in 1872 sought volunteers in Rarotonga to go as missionaries to Papua:
At one early morning meeting the chapel was crowded and I proposed that we should pray that God would help us to select the best man for the very important undertaking. At that meeting several old men stood up and said, 'Take us all. If we cannot learn the language to speak for Jesus, we can live for him and help the younger men in station work.' The enthusiasm was intense. Five men and their wives were selected and from all the islands we had numerous offers of service. Who that witnessed that 'setting apart' Sunday at Avarua, Rarotonga, will ever forget it? Old men and women, young men and women wept with real joy. That sobbed Amen of the setting-apart prayer of the whole assembly, I hear now.

(Lovett: *The History of the London Missionary Society*)

One of those five, Ruatoka, from the island of Mangaia, continued in service in Papua until his death in 1905.

One doesn't just go down to the ghetto and work with the Negroes. One moves into a certain neighbourhood and gets to know Millie and Tommy and Jimmy and Mary.

(Christopher William Jones: *Listen Pilgrim*)

One creature sustains another, one enriches the other and that is why all creatures are interdependent.

(Meister Eckhart)

For a worship group or a congregation: Discover who has friendships with people in other parts of the world. Using a large map, pins and threads, portray these 'rays' of friendship. Consider prayerfully whether new friendships might be forged by establishing a 'link' or 'twinning' with a church in an area where associations are scarce or non-existent.

Affirming Faith

The church has found it easier to say No
to a faith which is unorthodox
than to say Yes when it is adventurous.
The church has been quicker to say No
when faith is found outside itself
than to say Yes when it is clothed in strange language.

Yes, says Jesus, when the Roman soldier
comes as a last resort to the native healer.
Yes, says Jesus, to the sick woman who dared
to come through the crowd to touch him.
Yes, says Jesus, to the laughing children
when the disciples wanted to be serious.
Yes, to a penitent taxman who had defrauded the people,
Yes, to an erring woman longing for a new life.
The Lord says Yes to faith.
All the promises of God have their Yes in him.

Affirming God, may we share in this Yes to faith.

When we see the signs and wonders of the Spirit
amid ecstatic worship,

may we say Yes.
When we share the magnificence of a solemn mass
with its dignity and power of ritual,

may we say Yes.
When we sense a stirring of conscience
or a call to a new style of life and service,

may we say Yes.
When we meet those who stand on the edge of the church,
who yet know the attraction of the Son of Man,

may we say Yes.
And when you come to meet us
in a neighbour who is in need,

may we say Yes,
as you, affirming God,
say Yes to us.

Pray for: **The Middle East Council of Churches**

An old Arab proverb says: 'Pray to Allah, but first tether your camel.'
Those with no faith just tether their camels.
Those with some faith do both.
Those with a lot of faith just pray,
and those with complete faith don't do either.

An air of authority was another of Chalmers' outstanding qualities.
Stripped of all the visible symbols of power and prestige - a ship,
weapons, a large party - Chalmers had to rely on his own influence over
the Suan. Possibly they responded to him partly because of his white skin
which superstition or past history might have taught them to see as
another symbol of power, but much of his authority seems to have been
related to his own character and presence.

(Diane Langmore: *Tamate-aKing*)

You are goodness
and I find you
in people who do not confess you.
They lack your body
but speak your mind.

(Source untraced)

The history of religious experience is of women, men and children,
startled by an experience of 'holiness of being' to which they give the
name 'God'. Further, the ground of this experience is a response to
something given - before all human attempts to grasp for it. It is a
profound sense of entering into a relation within which all life is response.

(Mary Grey: *The Wisdom of Fools?*)

Affirming Presence

*When we hear the words of the risen Christ
in the last great commission, we meet the
universals of the gospel.*

All authority

Lord of all Christian tradition,
Lord of scripture and of all interpreters,
Lord of conscience and all morality
Lord of my mind, my heart, my will,
all authority is yours.

All nations

Lord of the complacent peoples
and Lord of the desperate,
Lord where freedom turns to licence
and Lord where oppression rules today,
to all nations your word is life.

All that I have commanded you

Lord by the well at Sychar
Lord on the mountain misted with glory
Lord in the temple courtyard
Lord on the way of sorrows
Lord in the dawn light in the garden
teach us your whole will for us.

Always

As the minutes fly in our busyness
As the hours pass in painful waiting
As the days reveal the consequences of our actions
As the weeks and years tell of our journey
And as our lives pass into history,
you are always our beginning and our end.

Pray for: **The Presbyterian Church of Aotearoa New Zealand (CWM)**

If Pentecost is, in large part, about receiving, then Ascension is, in large part, about letting go.

A wise and loving mother gradually teaches her infant to let go of her constant physical presence. The baby learns slowly - first through peek-a-boo games, then through longer absences - that when mother disappears temporarily, she has not abandoned him for good. He learns to keep an image and 'the feel' of mother inside himself, pending her return. Given a healthy early environment, we learn how to internalize (take within us) that which is important to our emotional well-being - and this is part of growing up and growing away. It also determines whether we are able, in our turn, to reach out to others ...

I wonder if this helps us understand the death, rising and ascension of Christ - followed by the giving of the Spirit? The disciples had gradually to let go of the particular personal embodiment of God in Jesus, in order to internalize him - find the Spirit of Christ within them. Not until Christ was within could they fully 'give out' in missionary endeavour.

(Kate Compston)

David Bogue in 1794 called for the creation of a society for mission: Perhaps we have not considered our duty resulting from that command which was directed from the supreme authority to every follower of the Lamb: *Go ye into all the world and spread the Gospel to every creature.* That has not yet been done. It ought to be done without delay.

(Lovett: *History of the London Missionary Society*)

Why aren't all parishes bursting to give away this life-in-Christ - instead of hoarding it in little church clubs? The more we clutch our resources in self protection, the more they will disappear. The more we give away our lives to others, the more God supplies the resources for mission

(Anne Hadfield, Presbyterian Church of ANZ: *NewShare*)

Genesis   11:1-9
Acts   2:1-11
Luke   11:1-13

The Gifts of the Spirit

Come, Holy Spirit, bring us love
and may we know our Father who is with us.

Come, Holy Spirit, bring us joy
and may we honour your name in all we do.

Come, Holy Spirit, bring us peace
and may we show the kingdom.

Come, Holy Spirit, bring us kindness
and may we share each day our daily bread.

Come, Holy Spirit, bring us goodness
and may we walk away from sins.

Come, Holy Spirit, bring us patience
and may we forgive every one who does us wrong.

Come, Holy Spirit, bring us self-control
and may we resist every temptation.

Come, Holy Spirit, gift us yourself
and may the kingdom, the power and the glory
come to life in our living. Your will be done.

A prayer based on Galatians 5:22
and the Lord's prayer

Pray for: **The Presbyterian Church of Korea (CWM)**

Pentecost is madness, non-sense, the breaking of the familiar rules of understanding, the revelation of a knowledge which had remained hidden. Wisdom emerges from foolishness ... Truth appears when the world we familiarly know is subverted, when its etiquette is no longer able to maintain the farce.

(Rubem A. Alves: *The Poet, The Warrior, The Prophet*)

The Spirit of this compassionate God has always been with us from the time of creation. God gave birth to us and the whole universe with her life-giving breath (*ruah*), the wind of life. This wind of life, this life-giving power of God is the Spirit which enabled people to come out of Egypt, resurrected Christ from death and started the Church as a liberative community. We also experience the life-giving Spirit of God in our people's struggle for liberation, their cry for life and the beauty and gift of nature. Only when we can hear this cry for life and can see the signs of liberation are we able to recognize the Holy Spirit's activity in the midst of suffering creation.

(Chung Hyun Kyung, Korea; WCC Assembly, Canberra, 1991)

For an all-age worship group: Chung Hyun Kyung accompanied her speech to the WCC Assembly (above) by a dance. Choose appropriate music and work out a sequence of movements that portray the liberating activity of the Spirit. This could be based on a Scripture passage (e.g. Ezek. 37), or on something more contemporary ... Offer the dance in a service.

As the dove gently settles on the tree,
receive the gift of peace.
As the flame rises free with light and warmth,
receive the gift of life.
As the wind moves and dances round the earth,
receive the gracious gift of the Spirit.

(*Mission Yearbook*, Presbyterian Church USA)

Treading Down the Evils

Let us remember God's promise:
I shall pour out my Spirit on all humanity

Where truth is compromised
to serve the mighty and the powerful,

empower us to tread down untruthfulness.

Where community is broken down
in the pursuit of relentless personal ambition,

empower us to tread down selfishness.

Where barriers are created
for the glorification of race, gender, religion or tradition,

empower us to tread down division.

Where the poor are kept poor
and opportunity is taken away,

empower us to tread down exploitation.

Where the just are killed
and prophets are silenced,

empower us to tread down oppression.

Where creation is destroyed
sold out as a mere commodity,

empower us to tread down blasphemy.

**Empower us, triune God,
to tread down the evils in our world.
Teach us your way of life,
fill us with the joy of your presence
and we will watch Satan fall.**

Pray for: **The Caribbean-North America Council for Mission**

Protect us, that we may not be entangled in evil, that we may not trip into shame ... Help us not to slip and get hurt ...

Grant that we might believe in you, be drawn to you, O God, heart of the heavens and of the earth, hidden treasure. You fill the heavens and earth at the four cardinal points.

(Part of a Mayan prayer)

Seasons' turning, seasons' learning,
all are held within your span:
times of growing, times of knowing
love in woman, child and man,
  calendar of calm and crisis,
  hurt and healing, high success,
  all the instants of our being
  now we bring for you to bless.

For we name you and we claim you,
Father, Mother, Spirit, Friend:
you are vision past our vision,
you are end beyond our end;
  all the circles, all the cycles
  of our little finite phase
  now we give into your keeping,
  trusting you through all our days.

(Shirley Erena Murray, New Zealand; stanzas 2 and 3 of 'God of Wonder, God of Thunder', from *In Every Corner Sing,* Hope Publishing Company, Carol Stream, IL 60188)

Everything that is in the heavens, on the earth, and under the earth is penetrated with connectedness, penetrated with relatedness.

(Hildegard of Bingen)

An Invitation to the Banquet

I invite you,
all you who seek security
in pieces of land and possessions
to come and sit at the table with those who have nothing to lose.

I invite you,
all you who seek to be comfortable
in the close circle of partner, family and friends
to come and sit at the table with the different and strange.

I invite you,
all you who seek power and status
driven by ambition without counting the cost
to come and sit at the table with the humble and gentle.

I invite you,
all you who seek conformity
and mindlessly live according to expectation
to come and sit at the table with the free and the dancing.

I invite you,
all you who seek stability
accepting a peace that is no peace
to come and sit at the table with the dreamers and visionaries.

> Christ, I want to accept your invitation,
> empower me through your spirit
> to risk, to share, to venture, to dare,
> to dream, to dance, to celebrate.
> At your great banquet of joy
> make me a worthy guest.

Pray for: **The Presbyterian Church of Wales (CWM)**

In the biblical story of creation ... the whole world is presented as one all-embracing banquet table. And this image of the banquet remains, throughout the whole Bible, the central image of life. It is the image of life at its creation and also at its end and fulfilment: 'that you eat and drink at my table in my kingdom.'

(Alexander Schmemann, *For the Life of the World*)

Companions are those who eat bread together.
(Latin: 'com' - with; 'panis' - bread)

Conversion to an awareness of our interconnectedness will transform and inspire the spirituality we live, personally and in common. The eucharist becomes *the* rite of exchange. The eucharist is the place where we glimpse what happens when the life of Christ encounters the structures of this world's order ... The eucharist is constructive of community or it is not eucharist. We will recover the relationship of the needs of the world, the hungry, the forgotten, the captives, to our commitment to become bread and solace and friend for one another ... Each of us must discern what solidarity with our brothers and sisters means in our circumstances and how we will express it. How we will stand with villagers and farmers in Asia and Africa, with prisoners of conscience, with abused children, with the unemployed, the lonely and alienated. We begin where we are.

(Gwen Cashmore and Joan Puls: *Clearing the Way:* En Route to an Ecumenical Spirituality)

Let us not die from poverty of caring,
        let us not starve, where love is to be shared.
Come, break us open to receive your healing:
        your broken body be our wine and bread.

(Shirley Erena Murray, New Zealand; stanzas 3 and 4 of 'God of all time', from *In Every Corner Sing,* Hope Publishing Company, Carol Stream, IL 60188)

God Is With Us

We are not alone.
God of liberation, you brought your people out of Egypt
and guided them through the vast and dreadful desert
to a land of promise and hope.
In those who break free from bondage,
who find the courage to become what they have not been before,
we see your hand, even today.

We celebrate your presence.

We are not alone.
Christ of compassion, you responded to the wounded and worried,
healing a desperate woman,
comforting an anxious father.
In those who refuse to give up,
who continue to care for the sick and the grieving,
the broken and the angry,
we see your face,
even today.

We celebrate your presence.

We are not alone.
Spirit of courage, you came from heaven like a violent wind
and gave yourself to Peter and John,
empowering them to speak boldly of salvation and life
to the mighty and the powerful.
In those who keep faith with you,
who continue to remind us of dreams once dreamt
and of beacons along the way,
we hear your voice,
even today.

We celebrate your presence.

Pray for: **The Presbyterian Church of Myanmar (CWM)**

Deprivation of many kinds can mean the haemorrhaging of hope and joy. Here are some stories from News Share about opportunities for arresting bleeding and coming into touch with Christ.

The Presbyterian Church of Myanmar started a new ministry of healing four years ago by opening the Agape Clinic at Tahan with financial help from CWM. It has been instrumental in demonstrating God's love and compassion in a tangible way by giving medical treatment to thousands of people. It is equipped with an X-ray machine, a laboratory and two power generators which are extremely important because Tahan has no electricity.

In villages there is often no paid work. People still have to survive. Our Church of Bangladesh Social Development Programme, with support from its overseas partners, provides motivation, through group formation, self help programmes, adult literacy, and low interest loans. Through rural community centres people are encouraged to raise livestock, grow vegetables, attend literacy groups and family planning sessions, and to participate in income generating schemes. It is an ongoing struggle and we can only try to give these underprivileged people some hope for their future and their children's future, against what must sometimes seem to be insurmountable odds.

Patrick and Frederick are twins from Mananjay on the south east coast of Madagascar. Their mother rejected them because her customs didn't allow her to keep them. Their father left the mother when he knew about her pregnancy. A pastor's wife saw the newborn babies by the roadside, picked them up and took care of them for a month. Then she called TOPAZA, a centre for bringing up parentless children. The centre took them into their charge. Now they are ten months old and in very good health. A French couple decided to adopt them, and now they are enjoying the warmth of a family.

Healing the Lost

We remember that so many people are lost.
Missing persons - the pictures in police stations
tell us of those who have left home without trace.
The disappeared - those in many countries taken
by the authorities and never heard of again.
Battered wives and beaten children - hidden
behind the curtains and unknown to the world.

Seeking God, so many are lost to us
　　　but not one is lost to you.
　　　　　　　　Keep seeking,
　　　　　　　　great shepherd of the flock.
We pray for the homes where there is an empty chair,
　　　a familiar face missing, and no news coming.
　　　　　　　　Keep seeking, good shepherd,
　　　　　　　　to restore the lost ones.
We pray for those wandering hopelessly in a city,
　　　lonely in the crowd, taken in for questioning,
　　　far away in a war zone.
　　　　　　　　Keep seeking, tireless shepherd,
　　　　　　　　to build fellowship anew.
We pray for ourselves, so often lost
　　　in our busyness, in the confused claims on our lives,
　　　tempted by our fears into violent attitudes.
　　　　　　　　Seek and find us, loving Christ,
　　　　　　　　and keep us in your light.
We pray for all who share in your seeking,
　　　all who respond to phone calls from the anxious and desperate,
　　　those who staff hostels and lodgings
　　　in the great cities of the world,
　　　and all befrienders.
　　　　　　　　In their seeking, may your
　　　　　　　　love shine and rejoicing begin.

Pray for: **The Church of Bangladesh (CWM)**

During the years of the military junta in Argentina, the police arrested many young people for political indiscretions, and most of them were not heard of again.

Every week on Thursday lunchtime there was a silent protest by the mothers and grandmothers of the Disappeared. Each wore a white headscarf with the name of the lost person and the date they were taken. They walked in a silent procession around the Plaza di Mayo, before the presidential palace. They had no voice, no party, no force, no public relations officer, no vote. But their steadfast courage was a candle in the dark.

(Bernard Thorogood)

There is an enormous age-gap in the church. There are some under 14s but the majority of people are 40+. Where are the others? Do they not need the church? Is the church door shut for them? Did their parents not teach them to go to church? Does their God not live in the church? Have we become an artificial flower that does not have a sweet smell?

(Sourendrow Mondal, Bangladesh; Reflections on the church in the UK and Bangladesh; *News Share*)

For a worship group:
God as a Woman Searching for What is Lost
God is like a woman seeker of the lost, deeply concerned about all the alienations we experience. God is with us as we search for ways to heal our broken relationships with our bodies, other people, and nature.
(a)   Pause to listen to what this symbol says to you.
(b)   Address God through this symbol. What do you say?
         How do you feel in speaking to God in terms of this symbol?
(c)   Then become this symbol and speak to yourself.
Close with whatever prayers arise in you.

(Kathleen Fischer: *Women at the Well*)

9 July

Ruth   1:1-18 (19-22)
Acts   11:4-18
Luke   17:11-19

Healing the Rejected

*In the time of Jesus leprosy was the fearful
disease which sent sufferers into seclusion.
There is still plenty of it about. But the
plainest modern equivalent is AIDS which has
brought a similar shock to our generation.*

Healing God, we praise you for the Christ
who, without fear, met those with leprosy
and gave them new life.
May that healing touch
reach the fears and darkness of our world.

Touch us, caring Jesus,
> to take from our hearts
> that fear which makes us keep our distance
> from all deep agony.

Touch us, caring Jesus,
> to heal that fear for ourselves
> which bars us from understanding
> mental illness, disfigurement and the approach of death.

Touch those, caring Jesus,
> who have been segregated, rejected, cast adrift
> because they offend our competitive society.

And touch with hope, healing Jesus,
> those who give themselves to combat
> grim illnesses and all that threatens life.

> **I am come that they may have life
> and may have it in all its fullness.**

Even so, come, Lord Jesus.

Pray for: **The Church of South India (CWM)**

'Ten were cured; and where are the nine?' When Jesus asked this
question of the only cured leper who had kept the appointment, the man
didn't answer. Prostrate at his feet, he trembled with confusion and felt
that being *the only one* was embarrassing in the same way as being naked.
Christ was waiting. Over the square there hung one of the longest pauses
in the gospel. Hadn't ten been cured? Why was the silence so endless?
Jesus was calling out the names of the absentees one by one and to each
he repeated his question: 'Where are you?'

(Luigi Santucci: *Wrestling with Christ*)

At the southern tip of India is a town called Neyyoor. For years the
missionaries in that area had asked the LMS to take seriously the need
for doctors, but there was some reluctance in London. Some regarded
medical service as a diversion from the central task of evangelism. But
eventually Doctor Charles Leitch was appointed. In his first report from
Neyyoor in 1854, he told of 5,138 patients treated in the year. More
doctors were sent and, by 1895, Neyyoor and its neighbouring clinics
had become the largest medical mission in the world.
In 1922, Howard Somervell, doctor, painter and Himalayan climber,
visited Neyyoor, saw the work being done, and offered himself. 'If I had
not then gone to India at the call of suffering, I should never have dared
to look God in the face, nor to say prayers to him again. I take no credit
for this decision and deserve none. I simply felt that my job lay in Neyyoor
and that there was no getting out of it.' He stayed in service for 30 years.
The treatment of leprosy was a major part of Neyyoor's ministry.
Sufferers came long distances to seek help. Many had been rejected by
their communities. Treatment, both with drugs and surgery, took a long
time, so the hospital tended to become home for leprosy patients. But it
was a Christian home which healed hearts as well as bodies. The work
goes on at Neyyoor and is supported by our prayers.

(Bernard Thorogood)

Lover of Life

Jesus, you are the resurrection and the life,
for life overflowed from you
as you met the mourners on the road.

We, too, would be lovers of life;
forgive us when we become the friends of death,
when we sell guns and tanks to the world's poor,
when our cut-throat prices reduce producers to penury,
when we forget human rights in search for a bargain,
when we boost tobacco sales and dump toxic waste.
Forgive us, and fill us with your love of life.

In such a violent world death comes in many forms,
an accident, a storm, a surprise attack,
a long war, a slow starvation,
and we are not saved by guns and barbed wire.
Teach us, giver of life, that your way is security
and your command is peace.

God of grace, we are caught in shadows and sorrows when a loved one
dies for there is a great gap in our lives and our homes. When a young
life is ended we weep for all the possibilities denied. Enable us to
celebrate the value of life, whether long or short. Help us to trust in your
mercy. Lift our eyes from the grave to the skies, from the pain to the
promise that you are with us even to the end of all things.

Pray for: **The Church of North India (CWM)
and the Church of Pakistan**

A Buddhist story tells of a young woman who lost her mind because of
the death of her child. She walked from house to house, asking if anyone
could heal the dead child she carried in her arms. Of course, no one could.
Finally a follower of the Buddha suggested she see him. He listened to her
story with sympathy and then said: 'To heal the child I need some poppy
seeds. Go and beg four or five poppy seeds from a home where death has
never entered.' So the demented woman set out, seeking a home where
death had made no impact ...
At last, empty-handed in the presence of the Buddhist master, she
understood the meaning of his words. And quietly she went and buried
the body of her child.

We cannot judge a biography by its length ... Sometimes the 'unfinisheds'
are among the most beautiful symphonies.

(Viktor Frankl)

*Letter from a Pakistani colleague to a bereaved father, after the death
of his young daughter from cancer:*
> I have heard the death of your daughter that she was died.
> Very sad, very sad, very sorry. God help you in your future.

If I could penetrate the dark dividing us
- I on this side of death, and you on that -
Where should I find you? You must surely be ...
Where flowers vibrate with colours yet unknown,
Beyond the spectrum of our rainbow arch,
And bird-song has a meaning now half-guessed ...
Where love and joy are almost tangible ...
It is all there - and here, and everywhere,
Had we but eyes to see Reality.
If you came back you would confirm it all.

(Muriel Grainger, from *One-Room Flat*)

Healing the Penitent

We love the drama of the gospel scene, with those
stiff self-righteous faces embarrassed and disturbed,
while the woman of the streets brings devotion and
generosity. But we have to ask, where are we in this story?

Unexpected God, we thank you
that a Samaritan became the model of compassion
so that centuries of tradition fell away,
that a penitent thief and a penitent tax-collector
received your word of welcome,
and that, when a woman came to Jesus
to honour and adore, she was lifted up.
We thank you for your open-armed welcome.

When we think that we need no forgiveness
        expose our shallow self-esteem.
When we stand fast on rules that we have made
        lead us into the greater law of God.
When we readily condemn the behaviour of others
        teach us to look below the surface.
When we welcome you with formal, frosty hearts
        excite us to tears of joy.

When we stumble home to you
        let us rejoice with the angels.
When forgiveness is the path to new life
        may we share the pain, the peace, the new creation.

Praying with CWM Churches 1995

Celebrate our partnership (see inside)

Wedding celebrations in Tuvalu

This leaflet can be used as a part of your prayer life, individually or corporately, within a congregation. Suggestions for prayer can be supplemented and updated by using the Worship section of *News Share,* available from your church offices.

Celebrate our partnership!

Join in the bicentenary celebrations of the London Missionary Society/Council for World Mission: 12th-14th July 1995 in London, UK. Contact your church office regarding local celebrations.

South Asia

Church of Bangladesh (CoB) gives thanks that the Church has priorities for:
- spiritual and social development;
- leadership development training;
- relating faith to work.

Give thanks and pray for Rev Baarthout and Mrs Gijsje Baak (RCN) who are engaged in theological education.

Pray for the social development programmes which seek to help people discover dignity and self-worth.

Church of South India (CSI) gives thanks for the 20,000 new converts baptised in the last two years. Also, for:
- the 135 new congregations which have been formed;
- the trained community health guides deployed in more than 200 villages with the co-operation of the local congregations.

CSI aims to give priority to:
- leadership training;
- the building and renovating of village churches;
- a development programme for Dalits;
- people affected by the environment.

Pray for:
- Dr Leslie and Mrs Betty Robinson (SCC) as they continue their work at Chikballapur hospital;
- Mr Johnson and Mrs Grace Ampalavanar as they continue their teaching responsibilities with EKT;
- ecological concerns.

Church of North India (CNI) aims for a holistic approach in achieving its priorities. This will include:

- faith and order;
- life and mission;
- concern about the wholeness of all human beings.

The CNI Council for Child Care is working to combat superstition in a part of Maharashtra State so that children can eat proper food. The Council is gaining the confidence of the people.

Pray for:
- the continuing success of this venture;
- the Communication Department as it organises workshops to encourage competence and confidence so that people can express themselves through different media;
- Ms Zena Das, Secretary of the Women's Fellowship, as she continues the vital work of raising the profile of women.

Presbyterian Church of India (PCI) is thankful for the 850 missionaries sent out to use their skills in different places. Also, for:
- the continuation of church planting;
- the nurturing of members through theological education, lay training programmes, crusade and revival meetings;
- the aim to deepen the faith of local congregations.

Pray for:
- youth activities within the Cachar Hill Tribes Synod;
- the building of a three-storey youth centre;
- the enthusiasm of the youth who are supporting three missionaries for evangelism in an area of Cachar;
- their efforts to raise funds to employ a full time youth worker in the Synod.

Building the youth centre

Europe

United Reformed Church in the United Kingdom (URCUK) is encouraged that:

- there is an increased demand for opportunities for spiritual growth through quiet days;
- there is an increase in the number of adults and young people associated with the Church;
- a growing number of churches have benefited from programmes to identify local mission and the stewardship of resources.

Pray for the Church as it wishes to:

- equip leaders and develop discipleship;
- consider a pattern of ministry involving the whole people of God;
- integrate children and young people more fully into the whole life of the Church.

Reformed Churches in the Netherlands (RCN) seeks more youth involvement in exchange programmes with CWM partners. Also, it is:

- eager to see what the unification of RCN and Netherlands Reformed Church could mean for a new enthusiasm for mission at home and abroad;
- looking for new possibilities of sharing CWM personnel;
- wishing to continue dialogue with other religions and cultures at home and abroad.

Pray for Rev Dineke and Rev Albert Ferwerda as she works with URCUK in the Inter-faith project at Southall, UK.

Presbyterian Church of Wales (PCW) has a high priority to continue encouraging local congregations in mission – both locally and globally, particularly as they wish to appoint more mission partners at home.

Give thanks for the chaplaincies in industry and as one chaplain confirms "I see my task as ministry amongst people at work attempting to show that the Church cares for men and women where they are".

Remember Miss Eleri Edwards as she continues to serve in FJKM with the Community of Sisters and for Miss Carys Humphreys as English Language Secretary with PCT.

Union of Welsh Independents (UWI) gives thanks for past achievements and contacts made through missionary work with friends in many parts of the world.

Pray with the Union as it:
- seeks to create a deeper consciousness within local churches of the mission challenges and to enable those churches to participate in that mission;
- seeks ways to find its mission role within Wales where many people are in need of the knowledge of the Gospel of Jesus Christ.

Scottish Congregational Church (SCC) gives thanks for varied ministries:
- the Easterhouse Community Church with wide ranging aspects of mission in one of the most needy urban areas of Glasgow;
- the Paisley United Church, a town centre joint programme with the Church of Scotland involving group ministry and consolidation of buildings and resources;
- the Livingston Ecumenical parish, a joint project in a new town involving four denominations and five worship centres, some of which function in local community centres.

Housing estate in Easterhouse

Pray for the continuing needs of these projects.

Congregational Federation (CF) gives thanks for its smaller churches. Also, for its:
- trained leadership due to the success of an Integrated Training Course;
- itinerant ministers in some areas who are giving assistance to churches who still have no minister or pastor.

Pray for the experience exchange visit with FJKM, particularly when young people will make a return visit. Pray for more involvement by young people in the decision making process of the Federation.

Pray for Miss Mary Pearce as she continues her teaching responsibilities with PCT.

Pacific

Congregational Union of New Zealand (CUNZ) In addition to overall support for CWM, individual churches within the Union are continuing to support missionaries from their own local congregations. This involves churches outside the CWM family.

Prayer support is requested for Chris and Joy Ponniah, the pastor and his wife from Palmerston North Church who have gone to assist a church in the Philippines as they:
- establish themselves in the Philippines and adjust to living there;
- grasp a new language;
- get to know, live and work with the people there.

Nauru Congregational Church (NCC) Give thanks for the witness of this small island Church. Please pray for the development of understanding about partnership.

Presbyterian Church of Aotearoa New Zealand (PCANZ) gives thanks that:
- several presbyteries are developing a specific mission focus;
- many congregations are meeting the needs of the disadvantaged in their community.

Pray for guidance as PCANZ:
- develops bi-cultural commitment to the indigenous people, the Maori;
- aims for new structures to enable Pacific Island and Asian congregations to work with their own cultural values.

Pray for Rev Fei Taule'ale'ausumai in her work as Tutor at St Andrew's Hall Missionary College, Birmingham, UK.

Ekalesia Kelisiano Tuvalu (EKT) seeks prayer support for the programme which has been established for the whole Church. This involves:
- priorities for youth and women's work;
- communication and media work;
- chaplaincies.

(see front cover)

Congregational Christian Church in Samoa (CCCS) is thankful for:
- the educational facilities which have been developed;
- new additional school buildings at the church-owned Maluafou College and Papauta Girls' College;
- successful reports about their missionaries' pastoral work in UCJCI.

Pray:
- for these missionaries in Jamaica: Mr Etisone and Mrs Henrietta Tinetali Gafa, Rev and Mrs Asi-Sagaga, Rev and Mrs T Faaleava, Mr Iaeva Lagaaia and Mr Alapi Eti;
- that people will be encouraged to develop income generating projects to assist with mission programmes.

Kiribati Protestant Church (KPC) More schools are needed. Give thanks that KPC is able to:
- establish a new Junior High School;
- educate students who passed the selection examination but for whom there was no room in existing schools;
- re-evangelise inactive members and encourage them to be more committed and active in God's mission.

Pray for:
- the involvement of young people in the evangelism programme *Every Home Kiribati*;
- Mr Martin Vickerman (URCUK) continuing to teach at Stephen Whitmee High School and his wife, Taara.

United Church of Papua New Guinea and the Solomon Islands (UCPNGSI) Rev Edea Kidu, Moderator of the Church, is happy for partners to know that the Church has:
- produced many clergy who serve at different levels of the Church;
- continued to establish new congregations and new forms of ministry;
- successfully encouraged women to participate fully and actively in the decision making bodies of the Church;
- continued to share persons with other partner Churches.

Pray for the:
- urban ministry for young people;
- ministry to youth, children, and women;
- chaplaincies in all government and educational institutions;
- ecumenical work carried out by Rev David Vincent (URCUK).

East Asia

Presbyterian Church of Korea (PCK) Pray with the Church as it continues to grow in understanding of partnership. Also, remember Miss J N Kim who is serving with FJKM in development work.

Presbyterian Church of Singapore (PCS) gives thanks for the continuing challenge of ministry with the aged and for the work which is being carried out by Rev Dr Stephen Tan. Also, the care and concern for the social and spiritual well-being of tens of thousands of foreign workers from the Philippines, Indonesia, India, Thailand and Sri Lanka.

Please pray for:
- the building of 'All Saints Home' with 200 beds for the elderly sick;
- the building of 'Presbyterian Home for the Aged' with 150 beds;
- closer relationships with the world church through mission;
- Rev Derek Kingston (URCUK) in his pastoral work and his wife, Lai Leng.

Hong Kong Council of the Church of Christ in China (HKCCCC) is making a serious evaluation of their programmes for work and witness as they try to re-define the role of their Church at this historical time in Hong Kong. Pray for:
- Rev Ng Paul Chun Chi, the General Secretary, and
- Rev Miss Lee Ching Chee, in their responsible roles as leaders of the Church;
- the people who are trying to utilise school buildings for local congregations to start 'church planting';
- theological training, leadership training, the establishment of relationships with the Church in China.

Street scene in Hong Kong

Presbyterian Church of Myanmar (MPC) rejoices! Youth ministry is very successful and encouraging. Give thanks that:
- more than 450 new members have been added recently to the Church, mostly from the Buddhist faith;
- women are making progress in every area of their ministry;
- literature work for communication is excellent and encouraging.

Pray with the Church as it aims to:
- increase leadership development training to cope with growing membership, youth work and women's ministries;
- have a mission thrust emphasising that the Church can reach out to people who have not heard the Gospel.

Gereja Presbyterian Malaysia (PCM) *Vision Twenty-twenty (Vision 20/20)* provides guidelines for growth in every aspect of the country.

Please pray for church leaders:
- to become informed about the policies of the government;
- to maximise that which will allow the Church to become integrated within local communities, as they seek an increase in church staff workers and ministers.

Thank God:
- for the many centres where worship is not held in a church building;
- that christian educators or teachers who are challenged will consider early retirement and offer themselves to be trained for christian ministry.

Presbyterian Church in Taiwan (PCT) rejoices that there has been an increase of 13 new churches. Also, that:
- there has been increased financial giving to overseas crisis and emergency situations;
- there is a greater exposure to mission opportunities abroad and at home;
- there is a greater emphasis on aborigine concerns;
- a women's ecumenical gathering attracted 2,500 people.

Pray with PCT as the Church aims to:
- work with *Year 2000 Gospel Movement*;
- nurture Christian lives;
- give expression to socio-political concerns for the renewal and strengthening of society, including political awareness.

Africa

United Congregational Church of Southern Africa (UCCSA) gives thanks for:
- the Pastoral Plan for Transformation in Church and Society with its contemporary understanding of *Hearing God's Word Today*;
- the Church, as it engages in a shift from resistance to reconstruction;
- commitment to development, transformation and empowerment for leadership, especially with youth and women, and in rural areas.

The UCCSA holds together churches spanning five countries – Namibia, Botswana, Zimbabwe, Mozambique and South Africa. Pray for personnel in Botswana: Rev Christo and Mrs Antoinette Weijs and their children (RCN) who head up the ecumenical work in Etsha, Rev Derek and Mrs Joan Jones (URCUK) engaged in literature and publications work at Gaborone, and Rev and Mrs Mackeson Mutale (UCZ) engaged in pastoral work.

Presbyterian Church of Southern Africa (PCSA) gives thanks for Murray and Shirley Smith serving in Lighinga, Mozambique where a mission station is to be created. Pray that they will be:
- guided by the Holy Spirit;
- accepted by the people;
- encouraged in their work.

PCSA is to raise a pro-active campaign for the awareness of mission in each congregation. Pray for encouragement and an increase in growth for contact with the worldwide CWM family. Pray for Rev Tim Sawyer, convenor of the mission work group.

United Church of Zambia (UCZ) gives thanks that UCZ wants to have resources to help them do practical evangelism as Jesus did – He prayed, fed, healed and restored people to complete humanity. Give thanks that:
- the number of congregations has increased;
- places have been reached which were not reached before.

Pray with the Church that the Spirit will guide them toward the best use of their existing resources. Encourage people to accept a challenge that may be set before them.

Churches of Christ in Malawi (CCM) praises God for the positive approach for:
- recently trained ministers;
- the fact that they can grind meal for fund raising and help the community by sharing the resources of the Church.

CCM aims:
- to educate their members about giving to the Church so that it can become self-reliant;
- to start development projects so that funds will be generated to help needy people.

Pray for Rev N C Chiwala, a young minister, who carries great responsibility as the General Secretary.

We ask you Lord to give guidance and wisdom to the newly elected office bearers of the Church especially the general secretary since he is young. Lord, hear our prayer. Amen

Church of Jesus Christ in Madagascar (FJKM) gives praise and rejoices for the:
- renewal in teaching methods for Sunday School;
- rehabilitation of two FJKM schools as a commemoration of the arrival of the first London Missionary Society (LMS) missionaries;
- creation of new areas for evangelism.

Pray with FJKM as it aims to give priority:
- for mission, evangelism and the training of evangelists;
- further rehabilitation of FJKM schools.

Remember Mr Stephen Wilkinson (URCUK) in his teaching post and his wife, Hardy.

Everyone lends a hand in FJKM's Environment Programme of planting trees

Caribbean

United Church in Jamaica and the Cayman Islands (UCJCI) gives praise and thanks for:
- the mission education programme with effective leadership for church and society issues;
- the service and development strategy with focus on inner cities;
- growing indications of readiness to send and receive missionaries. Please pray for Rev Christopher and Mrs Carol Baillie, Rev David and Mrs Jenny Fraser (URCUK), Rev William and Mrs Reah Numa (UCPNGSI), engaged in pastoral work and Rev Bedero Noga (UCPNGSI) engaged in pastoral and community work.

Guyana Congregational Union (GCU) rejoices in prayer as the advancement of the renewal process enabled:
- the two persons trained as ministers at the United Theological College in Jamaica to fill pastorates;
- two female ministerial students to be identified;
- Rev Tauta Gaga (UCPNGSI) received as a pastoral worker for two years.

Pray for the Union's plans for:
- lay leadership training;
- equipping local congregations for mission;
- staffing all groups of churches with ordained clergy.

Dear God, grant us the grace and strength of will to be your faithful servants and stewards in times of hardship. May your Holy Spirit grant hope through Jesus Christ. Amen.

A church congregation, Guyana

Pray for: **The United Reformed Church in the United Kingdom (CWM)**

This made a strange seizure on my spirit; it brought light with it, and commanded a silence in my heart of all those tumultuous thoughts that before did use, like masterless hell-hounds, to roar and bellow and made a hideous noise within me. It showed me that Jesus Christ had not quite forsaken and cast off my soul. And now remained only the hinder part of the tempest, for the thunder was gone beyond me, only some drops would still remain, that now and then would fall upon me. Now did my chains fall off my legs indeed; I was loosed from my afflictions and irons; my temptations also fled away; now went I also home rejoicing for the grace and love of God.

(John Bunyan: *Grace Abounding to the Chief of Sinners*)

A Jewish story tells how once there was a king who had a beautiful diamond, and he was very proud of it because it was unique. But one day it became deeply scratched and nobody could repair or remove the fault. Then a jeweller came and said he could make the diamond even better than it was before. The king doubted this at first, but finally entrusted the jeweller with the job. When the work was finished, the king saw that the jeweller had engraved a beautiful rosebud around the flaw, and the deep scratch had become the stalk. The diamond was indeed even more beautiful than before.

Compassion is hard because it requires the inner disposition to go with others to the place where they are weak, vulnerable, lonely and broken. Our first natural reaction is either to flee from suffering or to find a quick cure for it. But the greatest gift is ability to enter into solidarity with those who suffer.

(Henri Nouwen: *The Way of the Heart*: Desert Spirituality and Contemporary Ministry)

Healing as Liberation

Spirit of God, you set women free
to lead us in the ways of faith.
We thank you for the woman at the well
who gave Jesus a drink on a hot day,
for Martha of Bethany who recognised
the Messiah, the Son of God,
for Mary of Magdala, Joanna and Mary
who first told of the resurrection,
for Dorcas at Joppa with her acts of kindness
and Lydia at Philippi with open mind and open house,
for Mary, woman of courage,
mother of wonder and glory.
In them all you show us how tears
and love and new creation belong together.

Creator God, whose image is planted within all of us, we acknowledge
how often Christian tradition has failed to recognise the strength and
beauty of your image in women. As Jesus Christ set women free, so may
your Spirit set free our language, our worship, our church life and our
imagination to declare your fatherly and motherly care. We pray for all
who work to establish the full place of women in the Church and in
society, and so to celebrate that community in which all may be fulfilled.

May your will be done
and all your gifts be set free
to declare your love in Christ.

Pray for: **The Hong Kong Council of the Church of Christ in China (CWM)**

For the first 60 years the LMS appointed only men as its missionaries. Many went with their families and little is recorded of the witness of their wives. From the 1860s, long before ordination was possible, the Society began appointing women in their own right. Perhaps the example of Florence Nightingale in the Crimea inspired the Board members. First in each area were Miss Sturrock to South Africa in 1864, then Margaret Irvine to Madagascar in 1865, Gertrude and Louisa Anstey to South India in 1865, Mary Heward to North India in 1875, Sara Jane Rowe to South China in 1877, Jessie Philip to north China in 1884 and Wilhelmina Schultze to Samoa in 1890.

Following them came many women with outstanding gifts. As examples, we remember Mabel Shaw who, for 26 years, developed education for girls in Zambia, using village life as the model for the school community. There was Annie Sydenham, appointed as a doctor to Hong Kong in 1924, lifting standards of maternity care, enduring the rigours of internment in the Second World War, and then going on with her work with the same dedication. In 1932, Constance Fairhall was appointed to Papua as a nurse. She pioneered the care for leprosy and TB patients on Gemo island near Port Moresby and went on to minister to the rootless young people who were drifting into the town.

Let us praise women of faith - builders and sustainers of the family of Christ.

(Bernard Thorogood)

Of women and of women's hopes we sing:
of sharing in creation's nurturing,
of bearing and of birthing new belief,
of passion for the promises of life.
> We labour for the commonwealth of God,
> and equal as disciples, walk the road,
> in work and status asking what is just,
> for sisters of the family of Christ.

(Shirley Erena Murray, New Zealand; stanzas 1 and 3 of hymn from *In Every Corner Sing,* Hope Publishing Company, Carol Stream, IL 60188)

6 August

1 Kings   19:9-21
1 Peter   3:13-22
Luke   9:51-62

I Will Follow You Wherever You Go

Christ, you are calling.
In the poor,
in the sick,
in the hungry,
in the dying,
you are waiting for me.

Christ, you are calling.
In the hated,
in the hopeless,
in the helpless,
in the haunted,
you are waiting for me.

Christ, you are calling.
In the homeless,
in the stranger,
in the children,
in me,
you are waiting for me.

I want to follow you, Christ Jesus,
so when you call,
help me to hear your voice,
when you beckon,
help me not to look back.
In the face of the unfamiliar
strengthen my commitment
and make me fit for your kingdom.

Pray for: **The Council of Churches in the Philippines**

I leave aside my shoes	-	my ambitions,
undo my watch	-	my timetable,
take off my glasses	-	my views,
unclip my pen	-	my work,
put down my keys	-	my security,
to be alone with you, the only true God.		

After being with you,		
I take up my shoes	-	to walk in your ways,
strap on my watch	-	to live in your time,
put on my glasses	-	to look at your world,
clip on my pen	-	to write up your thoughts,
pick up my keys	-	to open up your doors.

(Prayer, Anonymous)

Mary Dudley (1750-1820) was a Quaker saint, who strove to discern God's will for her: it was an agony for her to feel strongly called to travel and exercise ministry, whilst also being the devoted mother of young children:

Having a disposition naturally prone to affectionate attachment, I now began, in the addition of children, to feel my heart in danger of so centering in these gifts, as to fall short of occupying in the manner designed, with the gift received; and though at seasons I was brought in the secret of my heart to make an entire surrender to the work I saw that I was called to, yet when any little opening presented, how did I shrink from the demanded sacrifice, and crave to be excused in this thing; so that an enlargement was not witnessed for some years, though I several times took journeys, and experienced holy help to be extended.

(Mary Dudley: *Journal*)

13 August

Exodus   **22:21-27**
Romans   **12:9-21**
Luke   **10:25-42**

Who Is My Neighbour?

I remember a time, Jesus, when I thought I knew it all.
My knowledge of you was sure,
I listened to powerful sermons,
I read many great books,
studied scripture,
discussed and argued.
There were no questions to which I did not have an answer.
That lawyer could have been me.

I felt for him, Jesus.
He came to you with such important questions,
but instead of theological debate you gave him a simple story,
an unheard-of story at the time.
Instead of the usual Priest, Levite and Layman story
(like our Englishman, Irishman and Scotsman)
you told him a story of a Priest, a Levite and a Samaritan.
It was the +faithless+ who showed love.
Maybe because he knew that rules, traditions, culture and knowledge,
no matter how important for support and shelter,
should never be an obstacle to love.
The Samaritan became a neighbour to a man in need.
How offensive, how upsetting to the lawyer+s safe and defined theology.

You upset me too, Jesus, with your stories.
You give me answers I do not want to hear
and you teach me questions I do not want to ask.
My knowledge of you is no longer so sure,
you remind me that it is not what I know that will make me act
but who I am.
Teach me, Jesus, not to define my neighbour
but to be a neighbour,
to be sensitive,
to be available,
and always to show your love and care.

Pray for: **The Reformed Church of France**

Churches in the Wessex and Southern Provinces have link or twinning arrangements with the north and south Normandy regions of L'Eglise Reformée de France.

Pilgrim ... take it for granted
that this is your brother.
Do not previously judge him ...
If he takes something from you,
give glory to the God that has allowed you
to be Christ in the world.

(Christopher William Jones: *Listen Pilgrim*)

I don't say he's a great man. Willy Loman never made a lot of money. His name was never in the paper. He's not the finest character that ever lived. But he's a human being, and a terrible thing is happening to him. So attention must be paid. He's not to be allowed to fall into his grave like an old dog. Attention, attention must finally be paid to such a person.

(Arthur Miller: *Death of a Salesman*)

If we say we do a thing for Christ's sake or for God's sake, it may sound and it can mean we do it not for the sake of the needy. It is like a woman giving a tramp some bread: 'Not for your sake, my man,' she said, 'but for God's sake.' To which the tramp replied, 'Then for Christ's sake put some butter on it.'

(Howard Williams: *Down to Earth*)

For an all-age group: Make a large map of the buildings surrounding your local church. Think of imaginative ways in which you can make contact with the people who live and work there: how can you be available to them? Pray regularly for your immediate neighbours, setting candles on your map.

20 August

Ezekiel 12:21-281
Thessalonians 1:1-10
Luke 12:35-48

God of Surprises

God of surprises,
when I think you are not present in my life,
you reveal yourself in the love of friends and family
and nurture me in your never-ending affection.

God of surprises,
when we think you are not present in our community,
you labour to make us of one heart
and cause us to share gladly and generously.

God of surprises,
when people think you are not present in our world,
you bring hope out of despair
and create growth out of difficulty.

God of surprises,
you are ever with us.

When the days go by and our vision fades,
keep surprising us.
When our hope dims and our patience wears thin,
keep coming to us.
Teach us to keep our lamps lit
and to be prepared,
that we may see your loving presence among us.

Pray for: **The Presbyterian and Evangelical Presbyterian Churches of Ghana**

As a result of a link with CWM and the Presbyterian Church in Ghana, Charles Ahwireng came to the Halifax Group of United Reformed Churches at the end of his community work training in this country. His brief was the relate the spare space in our buildings with the needs of the community. His research and vision released a great deal of potential and led to our churches becoming deeply involved in the needs of the community, not least in unemployment and job training. Currently we have 250 participants on government training schemes, covering care, clerical building and environmental skills. We give thanks that someone from another country and culture enabled us to see what God required of us.

(Yorkshire Province, URC)

We offer God the honeyed cakes of our Sunday rituals, uttering honeyed words of our heartfelt devotion, trusting that this action will keep God at bay for the coming week. This is a refusal to let God be the God of all things, who is continuously drawing us to himself in every breath we breathe.

(Gerald W. Hughes: *God of Surprises*)

When I saw and laughed at the oversized American pants sent as relief goods, I realised that I, too, might be doing the same thing: bringing an 'over-sized unfit' Jesus in the Immaculate Host to an uncomprehending people. Not that I don't appreciate Jesus in the Eucharist, but that having focussed perhaps too much attention on the Host, I failed to encounter Him alive in the tribals. After all, did I bring Jesus there, or was He not there already, waiting for me to meet Him?

(A Sister from Bukidnon, the Philippines)

I greet him the days I meet him, and bless when I understand.

(Gerald Manley Hopkins: *The Wreck of the Deutschland*)

People Rise Up

O God,
you love justice.
When a woman bent over by the burden of tradition,
of illness, of poverty, of expectation ,
stands up
 and warms herself in the light of the sun,
you smile.
For justice has come a little closer.
She has become what she was meant to be.

O God,
you love peace.
When a man
held down by the burden to compete,
to struggle, to conquer and to win,
straightens himself
and chooses to live in gentleness,
you smile.
For peace has come a little closer.
He has become what he was meant to be.

O God,
you love community.
When all of us
burdened by the strife for power, for wealth,
for independence and self-sufficiency,
turn to you
and learn to honour the ways of Life,
you smile.
For your commonwealth has come a little closer.
We have become what we were meant to be.

We thank you, God of Life,
in your presence we learn
who we are,
who we have been
and who we are yet to be.
Thank you, thank you, God of love,
in your presence we rise up
as your daughters and sons.

Pray for: **The Congregational Union of New Zealand (CWM)**

The gathering (the second World Conference of Indigenous Peoples, Aotearoa, 1991) is run by the people of the Kohanga Reo movement, a Maori grassroots programme of cultural and linguistic revival. What energy they emit! We notice a mood of purposefulness in marked contrast to much of what we saw among Maori people a dozen years before. What has happened?

To understand the shift, cast your mind back to the 1970s. The Maori people, 12% of New Zealand's population, were in a state of depression. In the previous two decades they had moved in large numbers to the urban centres in search of employment, better housing, health care and education. Separated from their tribal roots, battling to survive in a Pakeha (white) dominated society, Maori became increasingly marginalized.

In 1975 a study of Maori people's views was commissioned by the government ... 'We said that nobody was to speak of a "Maori problem" again. We were going to leave the problems aside and talk about the joy, the wonder, the beauty of being Maori.'

It was the beginning of 'Tu Tangata', the 'stand-tall' policy, a bold experiment in transferring initiative to Maori people. Women's workshops, small business enterprises, language initiatives, arts and crafts centres began popping up like mushrooms.

(Edward and Elisabeth Peters: in *For a Change* 1991)

Brother, if you see a Bent-Over Woman beginning to unbend and to straighten herself, at the very least you had better give her a little standing room, because ... that's *your sister* rising to her full stature - that's *God's kingdom* cranking up!

And, sister, if for whatever reason you are still bent over, and you think that that's the way it was intended to be or must always be, then know that you have been given divine permission to straighten yourself fully and to stand up. Only the Devil himself would say that **now** is not the time or that **this** is not the place. If your spirit is bent over, you are free to rise up! Let it be so, brothers and sisters! Let it be so!

(David G. Owen in *The Churchwoman,* 1979)

3 September

Exodus 23:10-13
Romans 14:1-9
Luke 14:1-6

The Challenge of Need

*All varieties of Christian mission respond to
what is perceived to be human need. Sometimes
this is so overwhelming, so blatant that we
cannot ignore or mistake it. But often we cannot
be so sure. The deepest needs may be undisclosed.
In this Gospel passage Jesus sensed both the sick
man's longing for health and the Pharisees' captivity
to the rules of religion.*

Holy God, you know our need,
not only what is on the surface
but what is deep in our hearts.
You know our inner conflicts,
our fear of being wounded,
our resentment at unwelcome truth.
God, in mercy, meet us in our need.

Holy God, you know our neighbours' need,
although we misunderstand their silence
or their intrusive noise,
although we treat the fence as a barrier
and make the closed door an excuse.
God, in love, may we meet another's need.

Holy God, you know the church's need,
so readily self-absorbed
and devoted to non-essentials,
so anxious to be secure
rather than to be spent.
God, in mercy, keep us alert to our need.

Holy God, you know the world's need
which we glimpse only in snatches.
You know the cries of the whole family,
lifting their eyes to you, longing for release.
God, in love, set all people free.

Pray for: **The Presbyterian Church in Singapore (CWM)**

The remains of pensioner John Sheppard, 69, were discovered in December 1993. He had lain in his flat forgotten by everyone for three and a half years. Brent Council only broke in because of a water leak. John's fate is not unique: a London coroner estimates that 50-60 elderly people died alone in London and remained undiscovered for at least a few days in 1993. 'Twenty years ago, an OAP with no friends or family was found dead after a few days and it made front page news in the national papers. Now it wouldn't make a local paper,' he says.

(Ben McDermott in *The Big Issue*, April 1994)

Christianity is, it seems to me, most interested in teaching people, but not interested in being taught by people. It speaks to people but it does not listen to them. I do not think Christianity in Asia for the last 400 years has really listened to the people. It has listened to its bishops, theologians and financial sponsors, but it has not listened to the people.

(Kosuke Koyama: *Three Mile an Hour God*)

Responding to the challenge of need often means doing something practical to help, or becoming involved politically to deal with the 'roots' of need. But more frequently than we might imagine, a truly enabling response is, not so much a doing-something-for someone, as simply a being-with someone. This, indeed, is what solidarity means: a readiness to travel voluntarily into the pain and mess of another's life and to be a companion there in those depths - suffering the same deprivations, feeling the same pain. It doesn't sound very 'useful' - but it can be a powerful means of helping someone back onto his or her feet - as this simple little story illustrates:

One day, Che Chow fell down in the snow. 'Help me up! Help me up!' he cried.

A monk ran over and lay down in the snow beside him.

After a while, Che Chow got up and walked away.

10 September

Proverbs   25:2-7
2 Corinthians 11:7-15
Luke   14:7-14

The Challenge of Hospitality

Jesus Christ, you are host
at the feet of life.

> **We respond with joy
> to your invitation.**

You welcome us to share
all the gifts you bring to the table.

> **We pray that we may not grab
> too much for ourselves.**

You question the affluent guests
who come with a love of display,
and you cherish the hungry ones
who long for your good food.

> **May we, too, hunger and thirst
> for the justice of the Kingdom.**

You call all the world to your table
to celebrate fulfilment, fellowship,
reconciliation, peace.

> **For all tables spread
> and all hungry people fed
> we rejoice with you.**

We remember the feast that is set in the heart
of the church where Christ, the host, is also the
food and drink. We confess that we Christians have
often fenced the table with human constructions
of law, and have divided the table according to
different Christian traditions. We pray urgently
for that unity which will bring us as one family
to one table in one Spirit, to receive the one
food which is Christ our Lord.

> **With heart and mind and will,
> we seek this unity.**

Pray for: **The Congregational Federation (CWM)**

On eucharistic discipline in Africa:
Participation in communion is in practice extremely limited because it is interpreted as reserved for the morally upright. Out of a congregation of perhaps 1000, fewer than a hundred would partake. The things that debar a Christian from communion are totally heart-rending. People want to be included. Those who can, spend the day before examining their conscience, putting things right, and in prayer. The eucharist can be a celebration of faith.

(John Poulton: *The Feast of Life*, WCC 1982)

In New Testament times, the household existed in Hebrew, Greek and Roman societies as a voluntary association of parents, children, servants and other dependents for their mutual benefit. It is not surprising that the household played an important role in the growth and stability of the first churches ... Whereas the household can be composed of misfits and outcasts, the family - whether nuclear or extended - excludes people who do not belong. Thus the popular concept of the local church as a family is based on its exclusiveness. It is time for western Christians to abandon the idolatry of the family and to explore the implications of the biblical metaphors of the Household of God and the Household of Faith.

(Marion Beales, Congregational Federation: *News Share*)

My house is not my house
if there's someone without a house
alongside my house.

The thing is that my house
can't be my house
if it's not also the house
of whoever has no house.

(A Cuban child)

The Challenge of Obedience

There are so many kinds of cross to be carried
that we never know what to expect.
> Christ, who walked the way of the cross,
> may each disciple be given strength to endure.

We do not know the price that others pay
as they seek to follow Jesus,
for you can't explain heartache
or evaluate betrayal.
> Whatever the calling may be:
>> to endure disability
>> to outlast disappointment
>> to carry frightening responsibility,
>> to be steadfast amid corruption,
> may each disciple be given strength
> to carry the cross with confidence and hope
> and find you walking alongside.

O God, who did not take away from Jesus the cup of suffering, but in Jesus drank it to the end, enable your servants to carry whatever is needed to show your love and justice in the broken life of the world. Amen.

We cannot name all the cross-bearers, but today remember those who have the long-term care of the sick in body and in mind, who often get tired and who may not be able to see a full recovery ahead.

> Spirit of endless compassion,
> your care for us
> is the support that all carers need,
> to transform weariness into patience,
> and patience into hope.
> Come, with strength and joy!

Pray for: **The Guyana Congregational Union (CWM)**

Writing from Demerara prison, January 12, 1824, to the LMS Directors, John Smith told of his conviction by the local court martial for having encouraged a revolt by slaves on one of the estates:-

> It grieves me, dear sirs, that I am now a useless burden upon the society. I have endeavoured, from the beginning, to discharge my duties faithfully. In doing so I have met with the most unceasing opposition and reproach, until at length the adversary found occasion to triumph over me. But so far have these things been from shaking my confidence in the goodness of the cause in which I was engaged, that if I were at liberty and my health restored, I would again proclaim, during the residue of my days, the glad tidings of salvation amidst similar opposition; but of this I see no prospect.

> Your useless but devoted servant, John Smith.

Smith died in prison, 6 February, and is remembered in Guyana as a martyr for the cause of the slaves.

(Letter quoted in Thomas Smith: *History of the Missionary Societies,* 1825)

23 August, 1944: Please don't ever get anxious or worried about me, but don't forget to pray for me - I'm sure you don't. I am so sure of God's guiding hand, and I hope I shall never lose that certainty. You must never doubt that I am travelling my appointed road with gratitude and cheerfulness. My past life is replete with God's goodness, and my sins are covered by the forgiving love of Christ crucified. I am thankful for all those who have crossed my path, and all I wish is never to cause them sorrow, and that they like me will always be thankful for the forgiveness and mercy of God and sure of it. Please don't for a moment get upset by all this, but let it rejoice your heart.

(Dietrich Bonhoeffer: *Letters and Papers from Prison*)

Bonhoeffer was executed by the Gestapo at Flossenburg, 9 April, 1945.

The Challenge of Love

The voice from the road

How restless I have been,
greedy, thoughtless, vainly wandering,
seeking instant satisfaction.
Then when I was desperate,
with all my resources gone,
I thought of the family, of safety,
and took the risk of the journey home,
wondering if the mood would be angry
or the door shut.

The voice from the field

What a strange kind of religion you bring;
it's not very suitable, not very rewarding,
for those who work year in, year out
to follow the rules
and keep the church going.
It's almost, dare I say it,
that you like the young sinner best,
and that's no way to run a church.

The voice from the doorway

But, children, haven't you grasped it yet:
that the very heart of my being is love?
that my love is equally for you all
so that you may live in my household?
that the lamps are always lit
and the door opened wide?
Whoever calls as my child
is already by my side.
How can I make it plainer?
You don't claw your way in by duty done,
or by donations given or by lectures read,
but only by waking in the night
and trusting that I am there
with open arms.

Pray for: **The Caribbean Conference of Churches**

Where the object of love is truly an 'other', the activity of love is always precarious. Between the self and the other there always exists, as it were, a gap which the aspiration of love may fail to bridge or transcend. That which love would do or give or express may fail to arrive - through misjudgement, through misunderstanding or through rejection. Love may be 'frustrated'; its most earnest aspirations may 'come to nothing'; the greatness of what is offered in love may be wholly disproportionate to the smallness of that, if anything, which is received. Herein lies the poignancy of love, and its potential tragedy.

(W.H. Vanstone: *Love's Endeavour, Love's Expense*)

I believe with all my heart that the Church of Jesus Christ should be a Church of blurred edges ... a Church of no walls where people can ask their hardest questions without condemnation and share their deepest fear without reproach.

(George Carey, Archbishop pf Canterbury)

If there is not a place where tears are understood,
Where can I go to cry?
If there is not a place where my spirit can take wing,
Where do I go to fly?
If there is not a place where my questions can be asked,
Where do I go to seek?
If there is not a place where my feelings can be heard,
Where do I go to speak?
If there is not a place where I can try and learn and grow,
Where can I just be me?

(Author unknown, from *Compass News*)

The day we stop burning with love
people will die of the cold.

(Source unknown)

Gifts

Because you have blessed us
and have called us to serve you,
we come to you.

Because you have given us the earth to care for
but we take more than our share,
we come to you.

Because you have given so much
but we worship the gifts rather than the Giver,
we come to you.

Because you called us to love our neighbours
but we fail to see their needs,
we come to you.

Because you have given us food and clothes
but still we seek to possess more,
we come to you.

Because you are the God of love
and we need your grace,
we come to you.

> **Gracious God,
> come to us and meet us on the way.
> You have given generously
> but we do not know how to respond.
> So help us to strive for integrity and faithfulness,
> love and gentleness,
> purity and endurance,
> that we may only and always serve you.**

Pray for: **Gereja Presbyterian Malaysia (CWM)**

Renowned Christian poet and lawyer, Cecil Rajendra, had his passport taken away from him by the Malaysian immigration authorities in 1993, 'because of his support for anti-logging activities through his poems'. Rajendra's publishers in London said 'he has written fearlessly and tellingly about our environment'. But the gifts of the prophet are rarely appreciated on home ground ....

(Adapted from *News Share*)

The world and our lives within it are the gifts of God, for which we should be grateful. Our gratitude and thanksgiving are expressed in worship, but in a more basic and elementary way they should be expressed in restraint. If we love God, we will love God's world. If we are grateful for God's gift of life we will not waste the capacity of God's world to support life. If we love God's world we will try to understand how it works so that we will not ignorantly harm it, like a child playing with a grasshopper. We will learn self-control before presuming to control creation - taking seriously the Buddhist meditation, 'Cut down the forest of your greed, before cutting real trees'.

(Herman E. Daly, senior economist with the World Bank)

The sisters employed a driver who was very poor .. They tried to pay him well, but it was always hard for him to make ends meet - he had so many growing children. They gave him things; they helped him in many ways. They couldn't pay him much more because the convent finances weren't too good. But in time the driver's situation improved. One day he came with four chickens to give to the sisters. He presented them to the Mother Superior. She said, 'Juan, for goodness' sake. I bet your children haven't had a chicken dinner for some time now. Take these four chickens for dinner tonight.' For the first time, Juan stood his ground. He refused to move, and he was very angry. He said to Mother Superior, 'Are you the only ones who can give gifts? Can I not also give you a gift?'

(Story from the Philippines)

8 October

Amos   6:1-7
James   2:1-9
Luke   16:19-13

Bright and Beautiful God

Bright and beautiful God,
thank you for our world,
a place full of beauty and variety.
Thank you for the winds and the waves,
the stars in the sky,
the changing of the seasons,
the animals in all their splendour.
Thank you, God, for this beautiful gift.

Thank you, God, for the gift of people,
men, women and children,
of many colours and creeds,
in different shapes and sizes,
with many gifts and talents,
all made and loved by you.
Thank you, God, for this beautiful gift.

Thank you, God, for the variety of life,
everything points to your love and glory.

So when we see what is different as inferior,
free us from insecurity and fear.
When we create new divisions because we do not share,
remind us of Moses and the prophets.
When we use diversity as an excuse to oppress,
help us to remember, loving God, your great command:
To love our neighbours as ourselves.

Pray for: **The Presbyterian Church in Taiwan (CWM)**

You saw the sun rising from the sea
I saw the sun rising from the mountains
We argued for a long time,
Until you visited me and I visited you.
We saw the different facts.
You say it's summer
I say it's winter
We argued for a long time.
Then you visited me in the South
and I visited you in the North.
We saw the different facts.
You say 'White is beauty'
I say 'Black is beauty'
We argued for a long time.
Then you saw the black forest in my country,
And I saw the eternal snow on your mountain peaks.
We agreed that the beauty of white is in its clear brightness
And the beauty of black is in its mysterious darkness.
Sharing - face to face - friends we shall become
Peace we will create
You and me.

(Dr. C.M. Kao, Presbyterian Church, Taiwan)

A simple lifestyle is not a panacea. It may be embarked upon for the wrong reasons. But it can also be meaningful:
- As an act of *faith* performed for the sake of personal integrity and as an expression of a personal commitment to a more equitable distribution of the world's wealth;
- As an act of *self-defense* against the mind-polluting effects of our overconsumption;
- As an act of *solidarity* with the majority of humankind, which has no choice about lifestyle;
- As an act of *celebration* of the riches found in creativity, spirituality, and community with others rather than in mindless materialism.

(Thomas G. Pettepiece: *Visions of a World Hungry*)

15 October

Leviticus   25:39-46
Philemon   1-25
Luke   17:1-10

As Big as a Mustard Seed

Loving God,
we confess that we have failed,
we have not been what you intend us to be,
we have not been what we want to be:

We would touch the world with goodness,
but we chase after our own salvation.
We would care for your creation,
but we squander it with little thought for those still to come.
We would meet the needs of others,
but we find ourselves reluctant to share.
We would stand for truth,
but we remain silent in the face of evil.
We would live with love and compassion,
but we take on the values of this world.
We would share our faith joyfully,
but we lack courage to trust in you.

We need you, God,
if we are to become who you want us to be.
Transform us by the power of your Spirit.
Renew our faith day by day
and make it as big as a mustard seed,
full of promise and possibility,
so that we may live with courage and purpose
and see the signs and parables
you have for us
in the world today.

Pray for: **The Reformed Churches in Croatia, Serbia, Hungary, the Czech Reublic, Slovakia and Romania**

The Reformed Church in Croatia, one of the smallest Churches anywhere, has only two and a half ministers (the half comes in from Hungary), only six fully active congregations and a few hundred scattered members. But it has historic roots and ministers effectively in a Czech village, two Hungarian villages, as well as the predominantly Croatian villages in Vinkovci and elsewhere. They are minority people, by faith and in many cases by ethnic origin too. They are not embittered or vindictive, even though many of them have lost so much. They long for peace. They plead to be remembered. They want to express their love and greetings to fellow Christians in other countries. They ask for our prayers.

(Malcolm Hanson, URCUK, *NewShare* 1993)

Churches in the West Midlands and Southern Provinces (URC) request prayer support for their links with churches in Hungary, the Czech Republic and Slovakia. Pray for the suffering peoples of the former Yugoslavia and of Romania.

Everybody can be great. Because anybody can serve. You don't have to have a college degree to serve. You don't have to make your subject and your verb agree to serve. You don't have to know about Plato and Aristotle to serve. You don't have to know Einstein's theory of relativity to serve. You don't have to know the second theory of thermo-dynamics to serve. You only need a heart full of grace. A soul generated by love.

(Martin Luther King, from *The Words of Martin Luther King*)

Alexander Creswell, watercolour artist, was commissioned by the Royal Collection to record the fire damage at Windsor Castle:
It was exhausting trying to draw in rooms which were so blackened, but moments of light came when I spotted little rivulets of molten gold leaf running down the charred timbers.

(Marcus Binney, *Times Magazine*, April 1994)

22 October

Judges   7:1-8, 19-23
Hebrews   11:32-12:2
Luke   19:11-27

A Cloud of Witnesses

Before you, O God,
we remember today the ones who went before us.
Not held back by the awesomeness of the task
the followed you with tenacity and joy.
Full of courage and trust they went to new places,
ready to stand and suffer with you.

Like a cloud of many witnesses
they stand around us.

Before you, O God,
we remember the saints of our day,
who do not live by the rigid letter of the law
but by the wild demands of faith,
always prepared to give more,
always ready to be turned inside out,
knowing that new ways can only be found
through risk and pain.

Like a cloud of many witnesses
they stand around us.

Eternal God,
we thank you for the witnesses of all times and all places.
May the stories of their lives show us the richness of your grace.
May they inspire us to look deep within our souls.
May they encourage us to take the risk of faith
and to serve you in new ways.

Pray for: **The Conference of European Churches**

This is the Week of Prayer for World Peace, and also Amnesty International Week. United Nations day falls on 24 October.

When artist Walter Herrmann ended up on the streets five years ago, he refused to lose his creativity along with his home. Instead, he began writing messages on pieces of cardboard to highlight the increasing problem of homelessness in Cologne. He tied the cards together to form a wall. Other people followed his example, adding messages to his. But the city authorities refused to let Herrmann leave his wall of cards up overnight. Undeterred, he took it down at night, then loaded the necessary materials onto his bicycle each morning, and returned to one of Cologne's busiest shopping streets to rebuild the entire wall.
The wall grew in both a physical and symbolic sense with the start of the Gulf War in 1991. Herrmann moved the construction to St. Peter's Gate at Cologne Cathedral where it became known as the Klagemauer fur den Frieden, or Wailing Wall for Peace, and was used by anyone who wanted to express their concern about the War.

The Klagemauer now consists of over 30,000 pieces of cardboard bearing messages written by people from all over the world and suspended from lengths of string which are tied to lamp posts.
Compiled in a variety of languages, they call for world peace, highlighting the plight of the homeless and campaigning against nationalism with its fundamental hatred of foreigners. New messages are added every day, old cards are removed and preserved and none are thrown away. The Klagemauer has become a famous monument - schools borrow the cards for class discussion, churches have used the messages in their services and there has been extensive media coverage.
Last September, Kazuo Soda, one of the 350,000 survivors of the Atom Bomb on Nagasaki in 1945, paid an official visit to Cologne where he praised the Klagemauer as a symbol of the 'protective shield against violence and inhumanity'.

(Christa Schneider in *The Big Issue,* April 1994)

The Word Made Flesh

Christ Jesus, full of grace and truth,
you lived among us,
as a man of your people
and a man of your time.

You are the word made flesh.

When many distance themselves from the church,
help us to see that it may be
because the church has stopped being with the people,
because it has sought to be on good terms with the powerful.

Help your church to know that it can serve best
when it does not set itself apart,
when it feels as its own all that is human,
when it suffers with those who weep,
when it is happy with those who rejoice
and when it welcomes sinners.

Christ Jesus, full of grace and truth,
you are the word made flesh.
May the church serve in your likeness,
may it bring light in the darkness,
may it bring hope to those who have lost faith,
may it walk in your footsteps,
may it be love in deed.

Christ Jesus,
continue to become incarnate in all of us.

Pray for: **The All Africa Conference of Churches**

I needed an embodied God, an experiential God, a liberating God, a life-centred God .... I needed a God I could explore and splash about in, rather than a God that was under wraps all the time, conservative and stiff .... I needed a bigger, and concurrently a smaller, more intimate, God .... I also needed a God that was suffering with, and giving life to the poor and the oppressed people in Asia. I'd been to visit women in the Philippines. I'd talked to women in Malaysia. I heard about, and saw, the poverty, the abuse and the cultural imperialism of the West. It shook me up badly. I needed a God that cared for these people ... Asian feminist theology helped me to find one.

(Marjorie Lewis-Jones, Australia: *In God's Image*)

We've been here a week already and we haven't done much except get to know the people and the place a bit. When we read about being partners in mission and ministry, through the Council for World Mission, we might have been forgiven for thinking it would be more exciting than this. But this is it. So far we are partners just by being here. For baby Hannah of course, being here is what she does best (being anywhere really), and she's probably the one to teach us all about it. Everyone seems to appreciate Hannah being here. On Friday morning, Hannah, Beatrice (who does our housework) and I walked to the shops together. Everyone wanted to stop and talk, and Beatrice introduced us to many people she knew, and quite a few she didn't, who all wanted to welcome Hannah in Zulu. Hannah smiled and laughed a lot. I nodded and smiled a lot too. So did everyone else. So far, just being here is fine.

(Janet Lees: Letter from Natal, South Africa, Jan. 1994)

For a worship group: The Incarnation is about the *being-here* of God. For us, just *being here* with others, particularly those in need (but also those of different cultures) - is often all that God asks of us. It is good simply to be alongside: available, open and receptive. Share stories of receiving this ministry.

Genesis   3:1-15
Romans   7:7-13
John   3:13-21

By Christ's Salvation

God in Christ -
You come to save us, not to condemn us:
    We praise your loving purpose;
You come to lift us up, not to hold us down:
    We praise your vision for us all;
You come to rescue humanity, not to deny it:
    We praise your human form in Christ;
You come to all the world, not to a favoured few:
    We praise your universal care;
You come to seek a response, not to impose a system:
    We praise your tenderness;
You come to be with us, not to argue:
    We praise your indwelling;
You come to conquer all our dying:
    We praise your constant salvation.

Although we have heard it so often,
it still amazes us, Creator God,
that you should love the world.
We, enjoying such beauty, colour, light,
movement, and diversity of life,
have yet treated the world as our playground.
We, knowing the richness of human nature,
have still crushed people by the abuses of power.
And when all the wonders of science are deployed,
we assume authority over the processes of life.
But you, Creator God, love the world
    in all its parts
    in all its tempests
    in all its sorrows
    in all its potential
with constancy, pain and renewing power.

Pray for: **The Uniting Church of Australia**

As God sent his Son, so the Spirit sends people. They are sent in order that others may be blessed and released and made whole. The mechanics of mission may become very absorbing, for every institution runs the risk of introspection, and the Church is no exception. The CWM may appear an ideal construction to be admired by all the structural engineers, but could fail to emphasize the sacrificial, imaginative, individual service that evokes a response to the gospel. People, therefore, must come ahead of systems, ahead of standing orders, ahead of the theory of mission ....

(Bernard Thorogood: *Gales of Change*)

Jesus, is this what you say to us today?
How blest are those who abhor easy pieties;
    the kingdom of heaven is theirs.
How blest are those who train in non-violence;
    they shall have the earth for their possession.
How blest are those who fast for justice;
    they shall be satisfied.
How blest are those who see enemies as human;
    mercy shall be shown to them.
How blest are those who live what they profess;
    they shall see God.
How blest are those who build bridges of reconciliation;
    God shall call them his friends.
How blest are those who show the outcast
      that someone understands;
    the kingdom of heaven is theirs.

(Peter Matheson, Aotearoa New Zealand)

Good News! Good news for my people!
Hear what is happening in the hearts of a people
who have begun to awaken,
See what is happening in the hearts of a people
who have begun to walk together.

(Creation Story: A Latin American Reflection)

In Christ's Constancy

'Before Abraham was, I am.'

What God was saying in Christ
God was always saying from the beginning
and will be saying to the end of all things.
The Christ-word is the eternal word;
the Christ-touch is there in the exodus;
the Christ-challenge is there in the prophets;
the Christ-wounds are there in the sacrifices;
the Christ-faith already speaks in Abraham.
So the cross is not a sudden discord,
out of key with the history of the universe,
but is all of a piece.
From big bang to last trump
the Word is creative love.

Patient God, as you are constant, may we be constant too,
not blown hither and thither by every emotion, by very doubt,
by every fresh teacher, by every pressure to conform;
but travelling through every day
with your light on our faces,
your word in our hearts.

Companion, Comforter, Breath of life,
for those who have remained faithful
　　　　through long periods of pain,
　　　　through years of disappointment,
　　　　through hard service in lonely places
we praise you, Holy Spirit.

Pray for: **The Church of Jesus Christ in Madagascar (CWM)**

Long periods of service have often been an influential factor in missionary endeavour, and in LMS history this is emphasized by family traditions of service.

The Box and Gillison families, both serving in China, are examples. But the palm must go to the Sibree family. In 1795, John Sibree was minister of the Rook Lane Chapel and was one of the founders of the Society. His grandson James was trained as an architect. In 1863 the Society appointed him for three years to supervise buildings in Madagascar. He felt so strongly drawn to the people that, when he returned to England, he studied theology at Birmingham, was ordained in 1870, and went back to Madagascar, where he continued in service until 1916. He continued to use his skill in architectural work, but also helped revise the Malagasy Bible, train pastors and lay people, travel widely, preach faithfully. 'Idleness was one of the few accomplishments for which he had no natural aptitude.' He died in a road accident in 1929, aged 93. Three of his children became missionaries. James Wilberforce Sibree served in Samoa from 1898 to 1921, and two daughters - Elsie and Mary - were appointed to Madagascar as teachers. Mary served from 1905 to 1926, and Elsie from 1904 through to the end of the Second World War. One family - and 150 years of mission history.

Lord, you have been our resting place throughout all generations.

(Bernard Thorogood)

I dream of a hope
that an altar of life
can be erected in everyone's heart.
And that the love of God can overflow to heal
all broken lives and distorted visions.
And the altar of death shall be no more.

(Elizabeth Padillo Oleson, 1991: War: The Altar of Death;
In God's Image)

19 November

Exodus   2:1-10
Hebrews   3:1-6
John   6:27-35

Through Christ's Food

It was Moses who prayed to God for bread,
and there it was in the desert,
fine flakes like hoarfrost on the ground.
'What is it?' they asked.
'That is the bread which the Lord has
given you to eat,' said Moses.
Bread of Life, give us today our daily bread.

In all the wilderness journeys of the heart,
in all barrenness of spirit
and when we are utterly lost,
Jesus offers food which lasts.
Bread of Life, give us this food now and always.

What is this bread from heaven?
It is Jesus himself, his presence,
healing, challenge, grace,
his hope for each one of us.
Bread of Life, may we take and eat so that you live in us.

For some, affluence has brought a food surplus
with much wasted;
then it is all the harder
to trust in the gift of heavenly bread.
Bread of Life, keep us hungry and thirsty for righteousness.

For others, a loaf is the most blessed gift of all,
to be received with thankfulness,
for it is the chance to live another day.
Bread of Life, help us to share - that all may be satisfied.

Blessed are you, Lord, God of all creation.
Through your goodness we have this bread to offer,
which earth has given and human hands have made.
It will become for us the bread of life.
Blessed be God for ever.

Pray for: **The Union of Evangelical Reformed Churches in Russia**

Shukhov took a look at his ration, weighing it in his hand and hastily calculating whether it reached the regulation five-fifty grammes. He had drawn many a thousand of these rations in prisons and camps, and though he'd never had an opportunity to weigh them in scales ... he, like every other prisoner, had discovered long ago that there was short weight in every ration. The only point was how short. So every day you took a look to soothe your soul - today, maybe, they won't have snitched any. He decided he was twenty grammes short as he broke the bread in two. One half he stuck into his bosom, into a little clean pocket he'd specially sown under his jacket. The other half, which he'd saved by going without at breakfast, he considered eating on the spot. But food gulped down is no food at all; it's wasted; it gives you no feeling of fullness.

(Solzhenitsyn: *One Day in the Life of Ivan Denisovich*)

Every bite of the black bread baked out of the corn grown in the war-weary black soil of Russia was a defeat of the terrible history within him and a reassurance against the uncertain future. All Russians ate far more bread than was necessary; and produced also a greater variety of breads than any people I have ever known. I saw shops in the great cities where, in order to cope with this craving, they sold more than a hundred kinds of bread of every texture, from white to brown and midnight black, from snowy puffs of twist-bread to poppyseed rolls and grey Minsk pistolets. But nothing ever equalled the black bread that was meal and reassurance enough in itself. The hands of the Russians present would all reach first for bread.

(Laurens Van der Post: *Journey into Russia*)

Bread for me is a material concern. But for me in relation to my neighbour's need, it is a spiritual concern.

(N.Berdyaev)

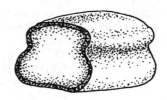

To Christ's Kingdom

*Pilate was not unusual in finding the Kingdom
of God puzzling. We often misinterpret it, through
the model of our human empires or by seeing it
as the Utopia of human desires. Yet Jesus
constantly used this phrase to declare his mission.*

My Kingdom is not of this world
We do not evaluate your Kingdom
by the scale of its success and power,
nor by the wealth in its treasury,
nor the glory of its buildings.
We see it in the Kingdom quality of life
in those who follow you.
Your Kingdom come, O Christ.

The Kingdom is among you
Now, in the present tense,
with no fanfare,
your reign touches our lives,
with no enforcement agencies,
but unshakeable authority.
Your Kingdom come, O Christ.

Yours is the Kingdom
So the poor enter their inheritance,
because of their need and your justice,
while the rich find entry hard
until they share your generosity.
Your Kingdom come, O Christ.

Seek first of all the Kingdom
with longing and commitment,
with intelligence and love,
with action and prayer,
with the whole of life.
**Christ of the cross, your Kingdom come,
to restore all creation to obedience
and bring us all as children
to the Father's house**.

Pray for: **The Congregational Christian Church in Samoa (CWM)**

Wherever, whenever, however the Kingdom manifests itself, it is welcome: in a healed body, in a restored mind, in a juster society, in a human heart that finds the power to forgive, in the faith and trust of a Canaanite mother, in the death and resurrection of the Messiah, in a new heaven and earth where justice dwells.

(Krister Stendahl: *Your Kingdom Come,* WCC)

The specific quality of Jesus lies in the fact that he does not proclaim that the Kingdom will come in the future. Instead he proclaims that it is at hand, that it is here in our midst by virtue of his presence and activity.

(Leonardo Boff: *Jesus Christ Liberator*)

The work will go on, enlargement and deliverance will come, until the earth, instead of being a theatre on which men prepare themselves by crime for eternal condemnation, shall become one universal temple of the living God, in which the children of man shall learn the anthems of the blessed above, and be made meet to unite with the spirits of the redeemed from every nation and people and tongue, in celebrating the jubilee of the ransomed world.

(John Williams: *Missionary Enterprises,* 1838)

> Unless you find Paradise
> at your centre,
> there is not the smallest chance
> that you may enter.

(Angelus Silesius)

Can't wait

"What does Advent mean?" the minister asked the children in the church.
"Can't wait," a little girl answered.

God of promise,
this is the time of "can't wait".
In the groaning of creation,
in floods and rainbows,
we long to know your promise.

This is the time of "can't wait".
In the love and the challenge
of the people we meet,
we long to hear your good news.

This is the time of "can't wait".
In the loneliness and hatred,
in the darkness of this world,
we long to see your light.

This is the time of "can't wait".
In the depth of our being,
in the forgotten corners of our heart,
we long to feel your presence.

God of promise and truth,
in this time of "can't wait"
we are still
and wait ...

Use this moment of silence
to prepare our hearts.
Use this moment to make us wakeful,
that we might recognise the signs of your coming
and know you.

Pray for: **The United Church of Zambia (CWM)**

An African theological student said: 'My people need to see the future coming over the hill. To put the vision of final things into the distant future is of little meaning to them.' The mission of Christ lives in the tension between the daily experience of 'not yet' and the compelling vision of creation's fulfilment.

> (*Mission: Commitment to God's Hopeful Vision*, Presbyterian Church of the USA)

Our sense of urgency is balanced by the requirement to wait - to wait on the timing of God, which we can neither predict nor force. And the poor of the world have much to teach us about waiting - waiting with hope, purpose, and active preparation for change; waiting without falling into despair. For activists it may be hard but necessary to thank God for 'the darkness of waiting' ...

> (Janet Morley: *Bread of Tomorrow*, SPCK/Christian Aid)

Increasingly, prayer seems to be a waiting - and often, a goal-less waiting: it is simply an end in itself. If some resolution, insight or peace comes, it comes as a gift, not as something I have angled for. I was at a loss to explain this to anyone until I remembered that the French for 'to wait' is 'attendre'. Then it became clear that waiting is giving one's complete and undivided attention ... to the present moment, to the person or situation one wants to 'hold in the Light', to the object before one's eyes, or the word arising in one's mind. To keep vigil is to be awake, waiting, attentive.

> (Kate Compston)

For a worship group: Share with one another happy and sad experiences of waiting. Looking back, how was God present in those times? Are waiting-times valuable in their own right? Practise using times of waiting (and being *kept* waiting!) as times in which to attend to the presence of God.

Messengers

We light a light for the past,
and give thanks for the messenger of Jordan,
proclaiming the advent of someone greater than he,
urging all people to prepare their hearts.
We rejoice that through the ages
the message has brought hope and joy.

We light a light for the present
and give thanks for the messengers of today,
their message like a lamp shining in a dark place,
calling us to watch and pray.
We rejoice that God is always faithful
and keeps calling for us.

God of our yesterday,
our today
and our tomorrow,
we light our candles
as we wait for the light of the morning star.
Help us to discern your presence
and to follow in the Way of the truth.
Teach us to live in expectation,
that everything we do today
is done in the certainty
of your Day dawning.

Pray for: **Ekalesia Kelisiano Tuvalu (CWM)**

The Church should light the sacred candle ... not merely through its preaching within its walls, but also through its actions outside the walls of the Church. We should dedicate ourselves to the task of reviving conscience and justice, which will bless us with a brighter and more just society.

(Stephen Kim Su-Whan, Korea)

(The prophet) stands in the middle of the crowd, but his roots are not in the crowd. He emerges according to broader laws. The future brutally speaks through him.

(Rilke)

The Churches' National Council in Kiribati said 'No' to the government when it was considering introducing TV recently. Their campaign was successful, but they wonder, 'How long can we hold out?'
CWM's partner in Kiribati, the Kiribati Protestant Church (KPC), has recently set up its own radio studio with funds from CWM and the World Association for Christian Communication, using the skills of its Communications Officer, Kaingateiti Maerere, a senior radio producer, poet and drama writer.
In Tuvalu, a tiny independent nation of only 8,000 people, video watching is an obsession. Imported films are often violent. CWM's Missionary in Tuvalu, Alison Gibbs, says: 'Tuvaluans aren't a violent people. Watching these films is going to have an effect.'
CWM's partner, the Ekalesia Kelisiano Tuvalu (EKT), has opened a video library which offers children's and religious videos and counsels parents on the use of videos at home.

(*News Share,* 1994)

Language not only describes but also shapes experience.

(Elizabeth Brimelow: *In and Out the Silence*)

17 December

Malachi 4:1-6
1 Corinthians 4:1-5
John 1:19-28

Wilderness

Wilderness is the place of Moses,
a place of no longer captive and not yet free,
of letting go and learning new living.

Wilderness is the place of Elijah,
a place of silence and loneliness,
of awaiting the voice of God and finding clarity.

Wilderness is the place of John,
a place of repenting,
of taking first steps on the path of peace.

Wilderness is the place of Jesus,
a place of preparation,
of getting ready for the reckless life of faith.

> We thank you, God, for the wilderness.
> Wilderness is our place.
> As we wait for the land of promise,
> teach us the ways of new living,
> lead us to where we hear your word most clearly,
> renew us and clear out the wastelands of our lives,
> prepare us for life in the awareness of Christ+s coming
> when the desert will sing
> and the wilderness will blossom as the rose.

Pray for: **The Scottish Congregational Church (CWM)**

The place known as Kuruman, in the heart of southern Africa, became the focus of mission to the Bechwan tribes. Work was started by James Read in 1817. He was joined by Robert Moffatt in 1821. The outlook was bleak. 'The prospect is neither calculated to encourage or cheer, but we labour in hope.' Moffatt struggled with the language. 'During that time we had not a friend in the whole nation, not an individual that loved or respected us or who wished us to remain.'

But they did remain and in 1829 there was a wind of change with crowds of eager seekers. The translation of Luke's gospel into Sechwana was finished. Schools were built and soon overflowed, though children were hungry. 'This is a land where the people may be said from necessity to keep one perpetual fast.'

David Livingstone joined the Kuruman work in 1841, but deter-mined to travel far into central Africa rather than stay in one place. Moffatt remained, believing that persistent teaching and example were needed. After 30 years' work, he completed the translation of the bible and continued in service until 1870.

The mission station then had difficult times, for the local population drifted away. But a new phase began in 1981 when an inter-church trust was formed to care for this cradle of Christianity among the Batswana.

(Bernard Thorogood: Quotations from Moffatt's letters in Lovett's *History of the London Missionary Society.*)

For (many) today the desert experience coincides with their increasing inability to relate to the traditional religious symbols that are embedded in patriarchy. As one woman said:

    The old answers that used to speak, no longer speak to me.
    There is a silence in me that as yet has no voice.

Some find help at this time by being introduced to a form of centering prayer, which Thomas Merton describes as

    a kind of praise rising up out of the centre of Nothingness
    and Silence .. It is not 'thinking about' anything, but a
    direct seeking of the Face of the Invisible.

(Kathleen Fischer: *Women at the Well*)

Sing for Joy!

Sing for joy,
God has come to live among us.
Sing for the joy of Elizabeth,
sing for the song of Mary:

> Our God will scatter the proud,
> our God will lift up the lowly,
> our God will fill the hungry,
> our God will show mercy to each generation.

Sing for joy,
God has come to live among us.
In the night of the star
God+s light has come to the world.
In the night of the angels and the shepherds
a cold and empty stable has become
God+s holy dwelling-place.
Sing for joy,
God has come to live among us.

> On this night we are filled with wonder.
> On this night we rejoice with the angels
> that in Christ you have come to us
> and spoken your Word of love and life.

> God with us,
> may our journey to your manger
> bring alive in us justice and righteousness,
> that we may worship the Child of Bethlehem,
> born among the poor.

Pray for: **The Church of the Palatinate in Germany and the Church of the Union (EKU)**

When we first met the Burgomeister of Frankenthal he was very hospitable and friendly. After having enthused over his town and its achievements, he recalled that he had been a prisoner-of-war in England. On Christmas Eve, a family came to the camp and took him to their farmhouse for Christmas and treated him as one of themselves. Their love and kindness have always remained in his memory.

(From a church in the URC Yorkshire Province)

Churches in the Yorkshire, Southern, Wessex and West Midlands Provinces (URC) request prayer for their link or twinning arrangements with the Palatinate Church in Germany - and with other German churches, east and west.

A Rumour of Angels
As for angels, I
know nothing of those with
porcelain serenity and
wing-borne gravitas.
But I have heard
certain hints,
rustlings and rumours; seen
the flickering of light
on shadowed corners, dignity
in suffering faces; felt
a sudden piercing stillness; smelt
in the dark night
scents of an
annunciation.

(Kate Compston)

The greatest testimonies that I have witnessed in the UK have not been the result of great thoughts, but of great hearts, and available lives.

(Peter Jackson, Southern Africa: *NewShare*)

A Guiding Star

God of all time,
who makes all things new,
we bring before you the year now ending.
For life full and good,
for opportunities recognised and taken,
for love known and shared,
we thank you.

Where we have fallen short,
forgive us.
When we worry over what is past,
free us.

As we begin again
and take our first few steps into the future,
where nothing is safe and certain,
except you,
we ask for the courage of the wise men
who simply went and followed a star.
We ask for their wisdom,
in choosing to pursue the deepest truth,
not knowing where they would be led.

In the year to come, God of all time,
be our help and company.
Hold our hands as we journey onwards
and may your dream of shalom,
where all will be at peace,
be our guiding star.

Pray for: **The World Alliance of Reformed Churches and the World Council of Churches**

I'm haunted that I may have seen the bird
that no-one else has seen,
yet not discerned the grace that wheeled my way.
Preoccupied, I may have lately heard
the song of fish, but been
unheeding of the notes that brushed the bay.
Blind and oblivious! it's not absurd
to think I've stroked the sheen
of precious gems, not knowing them from clay.
If I had glimpsed the star that signed the Word,
could I have read between
the lines of history hinged on that display?

(Kate Compston)

To evangelize modern societies requires not only the conversion of
individuals but the redemption of the values by which we live and the
structures which represent them. This is the toughest frontier for mission
today. It implies a style of church life which is distinctive, a sceptical
attitude to the mass media, a readiness to enter the process of politics,
a determined resistance to 'growth at all costs' and a commitment to the
disadvantaged sectors of human society. It means also the Church's ability
to restate the case for the reality of God, not in terms of the old logic,
but through the experience of human love, human need, human hope.
The missionary agenda will be about the alternative view of what makes
us human and also makes us one community of life on this planet.

(Bernard Thorogood: *Gales of Change*)

What we call the beginning is often the end
And to make an end is to make a beginning.
The end is where we start from.

(T S Eliot: *Four Quartets:* Little Gidding)

PRAYER HANDBOOK 1995 INDEXES

1. READINGS

COUNTRIES

CONTINENTS AND REGIONS

CHURCHES

Hong Kong Council of the Church
of Christ in China (CWM)   30.7
Kiribati Protestant Church (CWM) 19.3
L'Eglise Reformee de France   13.8
Nauru Congregational Church
(CWM)   16.4
Presbyterian Church in Ghana   20.8
Presbyterian Church in Singapore
(CWM)   3.9
Presbyterian Church in Taiwan
(CWM)   8.10
Presbyterian Church of Aotearoa
New Zealand (CWM)   28.5
Presbyterian Church of India
(CWM)   26.3
Presbyterian Church of Korea (CWM)4.6
Presbyterian Church of Myanmar
(CWM)   25.6
Presbyterian Church of Southern Africa
(CWM)   22.1
Presbyterian Church of the USA   7.5
Presbyterian Church of Wales
(CWM)   18.6
Reformed Church in America   7.5
Reformed Church in Croatia   15.10
Reformed Church in Hungary   15.10
Reformed Church in Romania   15.10
Reformed Church in Slovakia   15.10
Reformed Church in the
Czech Republic   15.10
Reformed Church in the Netherlands
(CWM)   30.4
Reformed Church of France   13.8
Scottish Congregational Church
(CWM)   17.12
Union of Welsh Independents
(CWM)   29.1
Union of Evangelical Reformed
Churches in Russia   19.11
United Church in Jamaica and the
Cayman Islands (CWM)   2.4
United Church of Canada   9.4
United Church of Christ, USA   7.5
United Church of Papua New Guinea
and the Solomon Islands (CWM)   14.5
United Church of Zambia (CWM)   3.12
United Congregational Church of
Southern Africa (CWM)   19.2
United Reformed Church, UK
(CWM)   23.7
Uniting Church of Australia   5.11
Waldensian Church in Italy   5.2

MISSION AND CHURCH COUNCILS

All Africa Council of Churches
(AACC)   29.10
Caribbean Conference of
Churches (CCC)   24.9
Caribbean-North America Council
for Mission (CANACOM)   11.6
Christian Conference of Asia (CCA) 5.3
Communaute Evangelique d'Action
Apostolique (CEVAA)   26.2
Conference of European
Churches (CEC)   22.10
Council for World Mission (CWM)   1.1
Latin American Council of
Churches (LACC)   12.2
Middle East Council of
Churches (MECC)   21.5
Pacific Conference of
Churches (PCC)   12.3
World Alliance of Reformed
Churches (WARC)   31.12
World Council of Churches (WCC) 31.12

THEMES

Affirming		May prayers
	Advent	3.12 ff
	Ascension	28.5
Bereavement		16.7
Bread		26.2; 19.3; 23.4;
		7.5; 18.6; 19.11
Carers		26.3; 17.9
Celebration		16.4; 25.6; 8.10;
		5.11; 24.12
Challenging		September prayers
	Christmas	24.12 ff
Compassion		19.2; 5.3; 4.6; 23.7
Death		19.3; 16.7
Desert, wilderness		2.7; 17.12
Dignity, standing tall		27.8; 5.11; 16.1
Discipleship		19.3; 6.8
	Easter	16.4 ff
Ecology		12.2; 19.2
Economics		29.1; 1.10
Empowering		June prayers
Enabling		26.2
	Epiphany	8.1 ff.
Eucharist		23.4; 18.6; 20.8; 10.9
Evil		12.3; 11.6
Friends		12.2; 15.1; 23.4; 14.5;
		13.8 8.10
Gifts, giving		29.1; 30.4; 28.5; 4.6; 1.10
Healing		July prayers; 25.6
Home, homelessness		2.4; 7.5; 10.9; 22.10
Hope		19.2; 16.4; 30.4; 25.6
		15.10; 12.11
Household		10.9
Identifying		December prayers; 2.4;
		23.4; 14.5; 13.8; 29.10
		(See also: Solidarity)
Incarnation		29.10; 24.12
Interdependence, connectedness		12.2; 19.2; 12.3; 14.5;
		11.6; 18.6
Joy		5.2; 16.4; 25.6; 8.10;
		5.11; 24.12
Kingdom		26.11
	Lent	5.3, ff
Listening		1.1; 8.1; 19.2; 3.9;
		5.11
Love		22.1; 24.9; 15.10; see
		also Compassion
Motherhood		26.3; 2.7
Mystery		5.2; 26.3
Participation		22.1; 26.2
Peace		12.2; 19.2; 30.4; 8.10;
		22.10; 12.11

COPYRIGHT ACKNOWLEDGEMENTS

Week 1   January 1st
1   Gales of Change: Responding to a shifting missionary context -
        The story of the London Missionary Society 1945 -1977 edited by Bernard
        Thorogood 1994 WCC Publications, World Council of Churches, Geneva,
        Switzerland published on behalf of the Council for World Mission, London.
2   Tools for Meditation, By permission of The Grail (England).
3   True Resurrection, (H A Williams) by permission of Mitchell Beazley, Publishers.

Week 2   January 8th
1   The Orthodox Way, Permission Sought.
2   The Meaning of Life, Life Publications, Permission Sought.
3   The Other Side of Language, (Gemma Corradi Fiumara), Permission Sought.

Week 3   January 15th
2   Gales of Change

Week 4   January 22nd
1   Gales of Change
2   Newshare
3   Mission: Commitment to God's Hopeful Vision, Presbyterian Church of the USA:
        Canacom, Permission Sought.

Week 5   January 29th
1   Gales of Change
2   The Upside-Down Kingdom, Herald Press Ontario, Copyright Owner Untraced.

Week 6   February 5th
1   Varieties of Religious Experience, Permission Sought
2   Peter Brock, in Your Will Be Done, Christian Conference of Asia
3   Stevie Smith, The Airy Christ.

Week 7   February 12th
1   Maria Benavides, My Mother's Garden is a New Creation, from Inheriting
        Our Mothers' Gardens: Feminist Theology in Third World Perspective, edited by
        Letty M Russell, Kwok Pui-Lan, Ada Maria Isasi-Diaz, and Katie Geneva Cannon.
        (c) 1988 Letty M Russell. Used by permission of Westminster John Knox Press.

Week 8   February 19th
1   The Wisdom of Fools (Mary Grey), SPCK 1993. Used by permission of the publishers.
2   Sithembiso Nyoni

Week 9   February 26th
1   Wrestling with Christ (Luigi Santucci), Permission Sought.
2   Good Housekeeping (Letty Russell) in Feminist Theology: A Reader SPCK 1990.
        Used by permission of the publishers.
3   Your Will be Done [Ed Alison O'Grady], Christian Conference of Asia Youth
        1984. Used by permission.

Week 10 March 5th
1   The Gold Crowned Jesus (Kim Chi Ha), Orbis USA. Used by Permission.

Week 11   March 12th
1   The River Within (Christopher Bryant) published by Darton, Longman & Todd.
     Used by permission

Week 12   March 19th

1   The Works of Ta'unga (Eds. R G & M Crocombe) Australian National University
     Press. Permission Sought.
2   Gales of Change
3   Your Will be Done

Week 13   March 26th
2   Every Bush is Burning (Joan Puls), WCC Publications, World Council of
     Churches, Geneva, Switzerland. Used by permission.
3   O Arco e a Lira (Octavio Paz) from The Poet, The Warrior, The Prophet, SCM
     Press 1990. Used by permission.

Week 14   April 2nd
1   The Upside-Down Kingdom
2   Highlight on Jamaica, Christian Aid 1990. Used by permission.
3   Fr Manny Lahoz in Suffering and Hope, Christian Conference of Asia 1978.

Week 15   April 9th
1   God For Nothing (Richard MacKenna), Copyright owner untraced.
2   Mission: Commitment to God's Hopeful Vision.
3   Story recounted in Marcus Binney's article, In the Light of Fire, (c) The Times
     Magazine, 2 April 1994.

Week 16   April 16th
1   True Resurrection
2   All a we a one, a Caribbean Notebook (Ed. David P Young).
     Permission Sought.

Week 17   April 23rd
1   Mission: Commitment to God's Hopeful Vision.
2   Suffering and Hope
3   The Poet, The Warrior, The Prophet

Week 18   April 30th
1   YouthShare
2   Hope in Romania by Julian Borger. The Guardian (c) 1994.
3   All a we a one

Week 19   May 7th
1   Bread of Tomorrow (Ed. Janet Morley) SPCK/Christian Aid.
     Used by permission.
2   Profile in Mission: The Reformed Church in America, Canacom.
     Used by permission.

Week 21   May 21st
1   Diane Langmore: Tamate-a King, Melbourne University Press 1974.
     Used by permission.
2   Wisdom of Fools

Week 22   May 28th
2   Gales of Change
3   NewShare

Week 23   June 4th
1   The Poet, The Warrior, The Prophet
4   Mission Yearbook, Presbyterian Church of the USA, 1992. Permission Sought.

Week 25   June 18th
1   For the Life of the World (Alexander Schmemann). Permission Sought.
2   Clearing the Way (Gwen Cashmore & Joan Puls), WCC Publications.

Week 26   June 25th
1, 2 & 3 NewShare

Week 27   July 2nd
2   Newshare
3   Women at the Well (Kathleen Fischer) SPCK 1989. Used by Permission.

Week 28   July 9th
1   Wrestling with Christ

Week 29   July 16th
4   One-Room Flat (Muriel Grainger), Outposts Publications. Used by
 permission.

Week 30   July 23rd
3   The Way of the Heart (Henri Nouwen), published by Darton, Longman & Todd.
    Used by permission.

Week 31   July 30th
1   Gales of Change

Week 32   August 6th
2   Journal of Mary Dudley quoted in Quaker Foremothers as Ministers and
    Householders, collected in One Small Plot of Heaven, Pendle Hill Publications,
    Pennsylvania. Permission Sought.

Week 33   August 13th
1   Listen Pilgrim (Christopher William Jones). Permission Sought.
2   Death of a Salesman (Arthur Miller) published by MacMillan Educational.
    Permission Sought.
3   Down to Earth (Howard Williams) published by Penguin Books.
    Permission Sought.

Week 34   August 20th
1   God of Surprises (Gerald W Hughes), published by Darton, Longman & Todd.
    Used by permission.
3   Suffering and Hope

Week 35   August 27th
1   Hence We Stand Tall (E & E Peters) in For a Change, Vol 4, No 5, May 1991.
    Used by permission.

2   Article by David G Owen in The Churchwoman April/May 1979.
Permission Sought.

Week 36   September 3rd
1   Ben McDermott in The Big Issue, April 1994. Used by permission.
2   Three Mile an Hour God (Kosuke Koyama) published by SCM.
Used by permission.

Week 37   September 10th
1   The Feast of Life (John Poulton) WCC Publications.
2   NewShare
3   All a we a one

Week 39   September 24th
1   Loves Endeavour, Love's Expense (W H Vanstone), published by
Darton, Longman & Todd. Used by permission
3   Compass News

Week 40   October 1st
1   NewShare
2   The City Gate, Summer 1992, The Reformed Church in America,
Canacom. Used by permission.
3   Suffering and Hope

Week 41   October 8th
3   The City Gate

Week 42   October 15th
1   NewShare
3   In the Light of Fire (Marcus Binney) (c) The Times Magazine   2 April 1994.

Week 43   October 22nd
1   The Big Issue April 1994

Week 44   October 29th
1   In God's Image, Vol 11, No 4, Winter 1992. Permission Sought.

Week 45   November 5th
1   Gales of Change
2   Your Will Be Done
3   In God's Image

Week 46   November 12th
1   Gales of Change
2   In God's Image

Week 47   November 19th
1   One Day in the Life of Ivan Denisovich (A Solzhenitsyn)
published by Victor Gollancz Limited. Used by permission.
2   Laurens van der Post from Journey Into Russia, published by
Chatto & Windus. Used by permission.

Week 48   November 26th
1   Your Kingdom Come (Krister Stendahl), WCC Publications. Used by permission.
2   Jesus Christ Liberator (Leonardo Boff) published by SPCK 1980.
        Used by permission.

Week 49   December 3rd
1   Mission: Commitment to God's Hopeful Vision
3   Bread of Tomorrow

Week 50   December 10th
1   Suffering and Hope
2   NewShare

Week 51   December 17th
1   Gales of Change
2   Women at the Well

Week 52   December 24th
2   Kate Compston
3   NewShare

Week 53   December 31st
2   Gales of Change

NOTES

NOTES

NOTES

NOTES

NOTES